"Terry Angelos's *White Trash* deserves acclaim and attention.

If any venue on the planet where I teach Family Therapy had the courage to allow it, I would use the book as an essential text. I'd make it required reading because the memoir offers a graphic window into several pivotal elements of Systemic Family Process.

It is all there: triangulation, the power of invisible loyalties, our deep connection to our place of birth, family process – how the generations before us impact our individual lives and how we potentially get to shift the future. It demonstrates the primal drives we each must fight, and how the search for survival and love can make or break us.

It challenges every stereotype about the darker side of troubled women and men and reminds us of the human ability to hurt, harm, judge and condemn. Above all, you will be reminded that grace, redemption, and the possibility of reconciliation, wholeness and love really is available to us all."

– Rod Smith, Masters in Science, Marriage and Family Therapy, Columnist and Speaker

mf

Melinda Ferguson Books,
an imprint of NB Publishers, a division of Media24 Boeke (Pty) Ltd
40 Heerengracht, Cape Town, South Africa
PO Box 879, Cape Town 8000, South Africa
www.nb.co.za

Copyright © Melinda Ferguson Books 2021

All rights reserved
No part of this book may be reproduced or transmitted in any form
or by any electronic or mechanical means, including photocopying
and recording, or by any other information storage or retrieval system,
without written permission from the publisher.

Certain names have been changed to protect the identity of the individual.

Cover design: Terry Angelos
Typography: Wilna Combrinck
Editor: Melinda Ferguson
Proof reader: Kelly-May Macdonald
Set in EB Garamond
Printed and bound by CTP Printers, Cape Town

First published by Melinda Ferguson Books 2021
First edition, fourth impression 2022

ISBN: 978-1-990973-38-3
ISBN: 978-1-990973-39-0 (epub)

For Kathleen

WHITE TRASH

by
Terry Angelos

Of all the things this book has brought me — you are one of the most precious — my dear cousin ♥
Terry Angelos
2022

"The cure for boredom is curiosity
There is no cure for curiosity!"
– Dorothy Parker

For my prince

INTRODUCTION

There is a wilderness embedded in my heart and etched on my soul. It is deeply imprinted on my childhood like ragged erosion scars the landscape. It is the taste of ripe mango juice running down my chin. It is the scent of dust and rain. It is the dull shine of a rifle in the bedroom corner. It is mud pies and mulberry-stained feet. It is a story of ears and lips cut off. It is newspaper headlines of missionaries murdered and terrorists slaughtering farmers. It is a song of patriotism howled with futility into the wind. It is the Boogeyman's face at the window. It is exhilaration and despair. It is lost innocence and the burying of a dream in a shallow grave. It is a place that is no longer written on any map.

Rhodesia.

It is the place that raised me strong-willed, fearless, curious, racist and entitled.

My heritage and its bloodied, soiled history that's entwined around my heart courses through my veins, pulsating with a mixture of pride and shame.

I am White. I am African. I am a descendant of White settlers, of tearoom owners, of tobacco farmers, of copper and asbestos miners, of British Military, explorers, exploiters and cricket players.

I am English-speaking but not actually English. My Britishness is second-hand, passed down like ill-fitting clothes, worn by others before me with stains that cannot be bleached out or stitched over with a patch.

White.

British.

African.

Half of each and none of all. A cultural half-breed.

I have impeccable manners. I am intelligent, bright and accomplished. Despite this, I have taken more than a few wrong turns, wandered off track and gotten lost down many dark rabbit holes. My recklessness, poor choices and lack of boundaries cannot be traced to the usual broken home, child abuse, abandonment, desperate poverty or drug addiction syndrome. That would offer a plausible explanation. You could put me in a cardboard box marked 'defective', or 'most likely to make a string of poor choices'. You could feel pity for me.

No, I am the first daughter of two devoted parents. Respectable, middle-class teachers. From the outset, I was destined for success in a white-picket-fence, 2.5-children family. A photograph my Catholic mother could be proud of.

Instead, by the time I reached 20, I had become a call girl. It was not forced upon me. I was not the victim of human trafficking or in a situation that gave me no other choice or nowhere to turn. I went in with eyes wide open, alert, aware and deliberate, with no one to point any fingers at.

There must be something or someone to blame? Surely something dragged me down the slippery slope into London's underground sex world? What was the catalyst to my aberrant behaviour? Why do I always take things too far? Why have I always pushed the boundaries? Why am I so reckless and unguarded? My appetite for life is relentless, obsessive, greedy, compulsive and dangerous. Curiosity killed the kitty. It's also what nearly killed me.

It's taken 32 years to feel ready to write down my story, to unravel a bulging mass of muddled threads, like one of those childhood maze puzzles. "Help Terry find her way out with a crayon." I never could find my way out. Instead, every twisted path led me to the edge of the abyss. The threads are memory scabs that I scratch till they bleed, shards picked from my brain and bones, caught in my throat, dislodged and examined. This is my search to understand me, the origins of my deviance, and the ingredients that created my recipe for disaster and redemption. This is the story of how I finally managed to uncover myself.

CHAPTER 1

MAGGIE

My earliest memory is a secret. It is the first time that I go to a place I am not supposed to go to and do something that I shouldn't.

I am a scrappy four-year-old when I wander away from our house. My mother is distracted with the frazzling demands of my new and unwelcome baby sister. She is always crying, her tiny face red and angry, little fists clenched. She already behaves like the middle child that she will one day become.

The heat of the day has simmered off as it turns to dusk. I crunch along the gravel driveway, following the swaying hips of Maggie to her khaya. I am unaware that I am crossing the lines of segregated living and separate eating utensils.

Maggie's khaya is a small cement block room with a tin roof at the bottom of our garden. It's called 'the servants' quarters', as if we are the Lords of a grand manor in our little red-brick house.

Her single iron bed is raised off the ground by several bricks. On my tiptoes, I can almost see the worn blankets and dent left by the memory of her body. The bed is raised as a precaution against the advances of the Tokoloshe, the African spirit demon known to have his way with women and bring a myriad of illnesses, bad luck and even death.

There is a small table in the tiny room, covered with newspaper and a few necessities like tea, jam, salt. I sit on the cool concrete floor in front of the gas cooker, crossed-legged like a skinny Buddha. The quietness of the small room feels secret and sacred. Maggie leans over the pot of maize sadza and gravy made from bitter, salty greens like spinach. She smells of Sunlight soap and her warm musky odour mingles with the cooking smells. It feels deliciously naughty to sit on the floor and eat with my fingers like she does. I watch how she rolls sadza into a ball with her fingers and dips it into the gravy. I copy her, eager to show her that I can also roll sadza and soak up the gravy.

Sometimes we have tea and thick slices of bread my dad calls doorstops. We "mix cement", taking a bite of bread and gulping a mouthful of sweet tea to mix with the bread in our mouth. This is bad table manners. This is how the Africans eat. "Don't eat like that, it's disgusting," my mother would say if she could see me now. I am not supposed to "mix cement" or "eat doorstops" like an African. But she can't see me, so I mix cement with Maggie, feeling happy as a pig in mud.

The light dims as the sun slips away, leaving flames dancing on the smokey walls. It feels like another home and Maggie feels like another mother. In these precious moments she is all mine and I have no comprehension that she has any other children, family or life outside our home and her khaya.

When my tummy is full as a fat tick, Maggie says, "Hamba, shaya wena," and I run home with no appetite for Shepherd's Pie or Eggy Soldiers.

It is the 1970's and generally, children should be seen and not heard. Dr Spock is instructing parents on how to raise their offspring by trusting their instincts and being flexible with routine. He is vilified as the founder of the permissive parenting style of Baby Boomers.

I play outside, mostly unsupervised in the daytime, happy to ramble around barefoot. Children roam around our neighbourhood, knotted together in little gangs. There is no need to worry, we are safe in the perimeters of our White community.

My mom says, "Come home when it gets dark." I always wander off. I am not the child that follows her mother around whining and complaining of boredom. I don't tug at her skirt or latch onto her. There is too much to do, to create and discover. My imagination is bright and vivid. It is like a kaleidoscope. Every time I blink, vibrant colours, ideas and wild images burst into my head. I am always exploring, building cities in dirt, climbing magical trees, making forts with sticks and straw. I play with dolls who for some reason are always dying of terminal and frightful illnesses.

I dress my Barbie dolls in clothes made from scraps. They live in pull-out drawers under my and my sister's beds and are characters in episodes of melodramas that we make up when we play with them. I am happiest outdoors. I love to ride my bike, sticking my legs out and freewheeling, the world rushing past my ears, everything blurring as my eyes water. Nature is a place of endless wonder, full of weird plants like the grass that looks like a man with green hair, the chameleons that change colour to blend with my T-shirt, insects like sticks and the ponds full of black slimy strings of tadpoles that magically grow legs.

We live on the fringes of a small town called Sinoia, a bastardisation of the Shona name for the town it was named after, Chinhoyi, and what it was known as before we lost the war. It is 115km northwest of Harare on the road that will take you to Kariba.

The town is unremarkable except for two things. One is that it is the birthplace of the Rhodesian Bush War. In 1966, seven freedom fighters fired the first gunshots at the Rhodesian Security Force near Chinhoyi. This was known as the Second Chimurenga, the start of the Rhodesian Bush War. In the year I was born, 1969, Sinoia had a population of 13,360 people. This number comprised 11,560 Black Africans, 1,557 Europeans, 206 Asians and 34 mixed race or 'Coloureds'. Whites were outnumbered 9 to 1.

Chinhoyi's other claim to fame is the world-famous caves on the outskirts of the town. The dolomite and limestone caves, just 9kms away, twist down into magical and otherworldly dazzling, surreal blue pools. The water temperature remains a constant 22 degrees Celsius, mystifying meteorologists.

Divers have never reached the bottom, estimated to be over 172 m. One of them disappeared trying, and his body was never recovered. We are terrified of falling in and disappearing forever in its underground chambers. At school we learn that it was "discovered" by Frederick Selous in 1887, and that it has a violent history and many legends.

Its traditional name is Chirorodziva, which means Pool of the Fallen. Tribal invaders marauding the area in the 1800's threw their victims to their death in its waters. It is said you cannot throw a stone across the Sleeping Pool, the sacred spirits that guard the pool will throw it back with a curse. We go there for lime milkshakes at the Tea Garden. We love to gawk at ourselves in the carnival house mirrors that distort our reflections into short, fat or long, ghoulish versions of ourselves.

We live in teachers' housing on a sprawling high school campus called Sinoia High School. Rhodesians pride themselves on the excellent standard of education for White children and it is reputed to be amongst one of the best schools in the world. It is an A school, which means White children only. We moved here from Bulawayo when I was five and had just started primary school. It is the place I will spend my childhood.

The school is built on an abandoned airfield. The district is surrounded by farmers and farm-related industries and the school is filled with pupils who board on the property. It is far safer to be at boarding school than on a farm. Farmers are on the frontlines of the bush war, vulnerable to roaming terrorists, caught in the crossfire, their homesteads resembling military bases. Guns are always at hand. Verandas that once hosted lazy gin and tonic sunsets are now fortressed with sandbags. Dogs and guards patrol electric fences.

I am glad that Dad is a teacher and not a soldier.

Sinoia High School is like an educational village. It is also the first co-ed boarding school in Zimbabwe. Stern matrons guard the boarding houses to make sure there are no shenanigans between the boys and girls. There are six well-groomed sports fields, multiple tennis and basketball courts, a gymnasium, an art room, a large swimming pool with two diving boards. There are tall pine trees, blue gums with silver leaves that smell of eucalyptus, granadilla vines, two fountains, a bamboo forest, dust roads, gravel roads, tar roads, gardens and footpaths.

This is my playground. There are teachers' houses next to each boarding residence. We live in one of these and have our own rambling garden. No gates or fences are needed to keep us in or anyone out. Fences are for dogs and petty thieves and would be useless at keeping out terrorists. The threat of terrorists is constant. We rely on the Rhodesian security forces, radio contact, patrols, convoys, landmine detectors and specially trained dogs. Our dogs, Mr Chips and Lassie, would not be very helpful. We have drills to prepare us for terrorist attacks and we know what to do if we are ambushed or invaded in the car, at home or at school. Our little town is a fragile island of safety, but five kilometres outside of any town or city is an open war zone. Everyone knows how to handle a weapon. Moms drop their children off at school with pistols on holsters strapped to their jeans.

Dad has a rifle and keeps extra weapons under his bed. He also has a panga, a Zulu spear, a knobkerrie, a machete and a bush knife. He is prepared for all kinds of attacks. It's not a good idea to disturb him at night. He also has a few homemade catapults on window ledges around the house. He reckons if you get shot in the head with a marble from one of those, you are lights out. Mostly he shoots at the monkeys who try to steal our fruit.

I have unfettered freedom on the school campus and can roam around the entire property. What a vast and glorious landscape!

There are a few places I can't go. I am not allowed to go down to the main tar road that passes the school from town and takes you to Karoi and Kariba. It's busy and dangerous for children to cross. I must not ride on the dust and gravel road that hems the school outskirts, dividing it from the bush like a badly sewn seam. I must not walk along the footpath leading to the African Location just north of the school. But when no one is watching, I go there anyway.

I follow the path trodden by 'muntu' feet to creep close enough to spy on these forbidden places. I take my bike to the pedestrian tunnel that burrows under the main road, reeking of human excrement. If I keep riding through the bush, I will reach Sinoia Primary School on the other side of town.

When I venture past the safety of our neat, trimmed lawns and cautiously creep through the pine trees along a path past the edge of the school property, I find a place so different from ours, it is like another country. Our White town is a land of bright swimming towels drying triumphantly on washing lines, obedient and robust hedges trimmed into upright rows and buoyantly optimistic flower beds.

Beyond our fences, sufficiently out of sight, is the Black settlement, referred to as The Location. Location, Location, Location! It's also called a 'compound', an accurate name for a compressed human settlement. This is a place of ragged clothing whimpering in the wind, of red earth beaten into submission, of fences made from mismatched poles, feebly trying to remain upright but falling over from their own futility.

I spy on this foreign land of blackened cooking pots on ashen fires, half-naked children with distended bellies and snot crusty noses, of scratching chickens, lazy flies and bored goats, of pungent smells and cramped living.

Africans are usually employed in towns or on farms. Some Africans live in rural villages on lands allocated to them as subsistence farmers. The rest are terrorists, I am told. Servants or savages.

I spy with wide eyes and a pounding heart, looking at a way of living so different from my own.

I race home before I'm captured by menacing black figures which are always lurking on the fringes of my childish imagination, cultivated by bedtime stories, African folklore, adult whispers and news reports.

The terrorists or guerrillas are called gooks or wogs but all the kids just call them Terrs. I am most worried about having my lips and eyelids chopped off by a terr. This is what the guerillas do to the villagers who won't give information or who are found protecting Rhodesian soldiers. They cut off the lips of the men and make their wives cook them in a pot and eat them. Sometimes ears too.

The Boogeyman, the Tokoloshe and the terrorists all merge into one terrifying monster that I am fleeing from. At night I lie awake in the pine bunk bed I share with my sister. Our curtains and bedspreads are covered with clowns. In the dark, the shadows cast by the moonlight and the smallest breeze transform them into a macabre spectacle of ghouls and witches that taunt me. I lie so still my body goes numb and I strain my ears for every rustle in the night. At any moment, a black face with white eyes and white teeth may appear at the window.

If I open my mouth to scream, will any sound come out? Will I be paralysed if I try to go to my dad and tell him there is a terrorist outside my window?

This is how I stiffly sink into sleep each night and dream of dark men coming to murder us. In the morning I wake to sunlight shining behind dancing clowns, forgotten nightmares brushed away by sunshine and the smell of toast.

CHAPTER 2

LITTLE SPIES

I am almost always with my best friend Paula. We are inseparable. She is the loveliest girl I know, and I can't believe she is my friend. She wears her light brown hair in two pigtails each tied with a bow. Her face is sprinkled with a few freckles and when she laughs, her hazel eyes sparkle. I love it when we giggle so much that we forget what we were even laughing about in the first place. All the adults adore her. She is diabetic and this makes her extra special. She gets injections every day and keeps a roll of Life Savers sweets in her pocket for emergencies. I am scrawny, olive-skinned and boyish. My straight black hair is shaped in some version of a bad pageboy haircut. No one believes she is naughty, so I am the bad influence when we get into trouble.

We are the most suspicious ten-year-old girls in the town. Our suspicions are fuelled by reading Nancy Drew and the Hardy Boys and surreptitiously listening to snippets of adult conversations about the war that we collect like scraps under the dinner table. We regard everyone on the High School Campus as a possible suspect, speculating on their double lives and hidden agendas. We wander along the dusty corridors and empty school yards with our 'eye-spy' little eyes, creeping around corners and tailing people, testing our ability to follow them unnoticed. We duck behind trees and shrubs, scratching in the dirt for clues, in discarded love letters and behind school classrooms. We peek into empty cars to discover couples entwined in sweaty, furtive kisses and rat out boys smoking illegally. Everyone is guilty until proven innocent.

One day, while skirting along the scrubby bushes on the outskirts of the school, we stumble upon a mysterious figure. Our snotty detective noses have picked up the scent of acrid smoke coming from behind the new squash courts. It's not the earthy smoke of a bush fire, or the meaty smell of a home braai. It is the slow smouldering smoke that carries the odour of its inhabitant, charred mealies, sadza and bush tea. We creep closer, hobbling on the gravel, our backs to the newly painted white walls, leaving our own dusty handprints behind as evidence.

We peek around the wall and see a dishevelled spectre who looks like he has been spat out of the bush. He is an elderly Black man wearing crumpled clothes splattered with paint stains. He stands in front of a small shack roughly assembled from sheets of corrugated roofing and other building rubble. In the bush, shacks pop up like mushrooms and vanish again, leaving behind blackened earth. This is not the Bush or 'The Location'. He is not a 'garden boy' or 'house boy', as he is unsupervised and living in an inappropriate place. A Black man cannot just build a shack on the school property. It's a tasty mystery for us to gnaw on.

We march boldly up to him and ask who he is and what he is doing. He mumbles in Shona looking at his feet. We decide to infiltrate his life like undercover agents and observe his comings and goings. We start with a thorough inspection of his shack. He looks puzzled as two little White madams walk into his life uninvited.

We will spy on him while at the same time doing good deeds, as White folks do. It must be genetically wired for us to interfere and think we know better. We investigate all corners of his shack and his belongings and prepare a to-do list.

The timing is perfect as we have just started our summer holiday.

First, we sweep his yard with his homemade brush of stiff grass tied in a bunch with twine. Next, we set off to gather dried grass to make a mattress for his bed. Sheets of tattered cardboard will not do. His bed is a wonky piece of metal balanced on four empty paint tins. We lay the straw down and cover it with a rough grey blanket that we find amongst his meagre belongings. We potter around happily, rearranging things and tidying up. We are buoyant with the thrill of adventure, flushed from our efforts and impressed with our progress. Madala is perched on a rock with a look of resignation and mild amusement. Every now and again he mutters something under his breath in Shona and scratches his head.

The rest of our holiday is spent carrying an assortment of supplies that we have raided from our homes up to Madala's shack. We act out an odd reverse parody of play house cleaning and cooking for the elderly Black man. To accumulate supplies for our project, we pretend to go on picnics, packing sandwiches and fruit, or we pilfer potatoes, butter, eggs and leftovers, hiding them under our grubby T-shirts. Small daily thefts accrue as we set about our secret project. Blankets, pillows, cups, plates, old shoes, shirts and cooking utensils are taken up the hill and behind the squash courts as if little by little an army of ants has carried them away.

We cook him breakfast and make terrible stews from our odd mix of stolen supplies and sit by the open fire with Madala, drinking tea from tin cups. We feel pleased with all we have done to help him. We would like to wash and iron his rumpled, smokey clothes but a missing iron would be noticed, and someone would be fired.

We have still not solved the mystery of who he is and why he is here. Although he seems harmless, he could be here as a spy for the terrorists or perhaps he was captured by a terrorist gang but managed to escape and is hiding out here. We are ever alert to the terrifying possibility we may encounter a terrorist around the corner.

The missing groceries have not gone unnoticed. Paula's mother eventually confronts Champion, her male housekeeper and cook. Who else could have pilfered the groceries and household items?

Champion is considered 'part of the family'. This is typical of the relationship between the 'Madams' and their servants. Like all 'house boys' and 'maids', he is well trained, like a good and obedient pet. Fetch, stay, go. House help should know just enough English to follow commands and carry out household duties, but never enough to be too intelligent or question their place in life. Insolence and stealing will not be tolerated. Blacks ought to know that we have their best interests at heart. Prime Minister Ian Smith once proudly boasted that "our Blacks are the happiest Blacks in Africa". Mr Smith also believes that Black people are unfit to govern. The country would descend into communist chaos if they did. Our beautiful Rhodesia would go to the dogs. White supremacists would then point self-righteous white fingers at Zimbabwe and say, "We told you so." It never occurs to us that a country governed by oppression and racism, with an infrastructure that benefits only 3% of its population, is an unstable foundation waiting to collapse. The terrorists will topple a regime and the implosion is inevitable. The grass is only greener on our manicured gardens.

I am ashamed our charity to one man may incriminate another. In our naivety and entitlement, we do not see the harm until we hear the accusations. The confused Champion is assumed guilty till proven otherwise. This is my first experience of a moral dilemma and I confide in the Italian nuns at St Agnes Roman Catholic

Church. They are a clutch of short, round, holy penguins with rosy cheeks. "Is it wrong to steal to feed a beggar?" I ask. "Indeed, it is," is the reply. I will have to confess my sin in the musty confession cupboard to Father Anthony. I feel bad about stealing but mostly I feel bad about getting Champion into trouble.

One day we go to check up on the old man and he has vanished, leaving just a burnt patch where the shack was, some rusty tins and no evidence of the reason for his disappearance. We speculate for days about whether he was murdered or abducted. If we were better sleuths, the paint tins and paint-splattered clothing should have been clues enough to realise that his piece job was to paint the squash courts. He has simply left because the job is finished.

CHAPTER 3

DEFORMITIES IN JARS

The Tanners are the most patriotic family I know. I am friends with their eldest daughter. They have three girls, all with beautiful names: Charlotte, Emily and Sarah, but they are quite unruly with tangled hair and boyish clothing. Their father owns a fitting and turning factory on the outskirts of the town and sometimes, after school, I spend the afternoon there.

Mr Tanner is tall, quiet and gentle, always in grease-stained blue overalls. He washes his hands in special soap to remove the grease, but it doesn't work, and the dark stains remain under his nails and in the creases of his skin.

Mrs Tanner is always perched in the front office, buried under mounds of gritty paperwork. She moves in large silent strides and has the uncanny ability to appear out of nowhere at the exact moment you are about to do something that you shouldn't.

We scoot around the factory on a variety of contraptions: bikes, scooters, push-carts, all fashioned from welding odds and ends together like toys from a dystopian future. We have a circuit of sorts in the factory, a smooth path between screeching, pounding machinery, flanked with mounds of shiny metallic shards and sawdust shavings. We must not touch the machinery which could turn our fingers into minced meat. We must be extremely careful not to bump or distract the African workers operating the machinery while we hurtle around on our contraptions. They must be vigilant while they work, or their fingers will also be minced.

The coolest thing the Tanners have is a hybrid vehicle resembling a golf cart, with the wheels of a jeep. It is painted a glossy enamel white which is stained with greasy fingerprints. There are bumpy scars where it has been welded together. It has no windows or doors. We are obsessed with trying to push start it when Mrs Tanner is not looking. Sometimes we succeed and then jump out in a panic to stop it crashing into the fence.

When it's time to go home, Mr and Mrs Tanner, kids and friends – usually about ten people – pile onto the odd golf cart contraption and ride home, hurtling through the town. Mr Tanner's head touches the roof, his knees folded up to his ears. As we bounce along, our eyes smarting, hair whipping around our faces, we sing patriotic war songs, and the wind steals the words from our mouths, flinging them at people that we pass by. The late afternoon sun dips behind the trees, leaving a chill, and my scrawny legs pucker with goosebumps.

We sing:
"We're all Rhodesians
And we'll fight through thick and thin
We'll keep our land a free land
Stop the enemy coming in
We'll keep them north of the Zambezi
'Till that river's running dry
This mighty land will prosper
For Rhodesians never die."

As I sing, my little heart thumps with a fierce loyalty for all I love in my small universe. I sing as if I can, by sheer will, keep everything unchanged. I sing with the purest sincerity, not knowing the irony and futility of the words.

I know absolutely nothing of the realities and atrocities of war. I have no framework for it other than the bias of my birthright, my white skin – the privilege stamping its superiority on every aspect of my life. There is no inkling of being wrong or bad or immoral. We are White but we never think of ourselves as White supremacist. White supremacists are Nazi skinheads who wear white vests and tattoo the swastika on their arms. We are decent people. Good citizens.

War has a way of illuminating life, bringing it into razor-sharp focus, which is perhaps why my childhood memories are so vivid. They are tinged with a strangely idyllic hysteria and happy madness. There are fragments that are so pristinely preserved, it is as if they were captured and bottled in jars and labelled with brown tags and string.

When we went to the Bulawayo Natural History Museum, my favourite display was the curiosities, specimens held captive in formaldehyde for us to gaze upon their deformities. Two-headed frogs, a stillborn baby elephant, conjoined twin rabbits and other oddities. It is not only their strangeness that fascinates me, but also because they remain suspended in liquid, unborn, unchanged.

My own memories are like stillborn creatures, incompletely formed and frozen in time, strangely deformed through my own lens or magnified as if under a microscope, every detail sharply focused. Some are sweet specimens, like the smell of dirt and the perfume of sweet peas. Some are sickening, twisting my gut in shame and regret. My memory – a mental museum filled with frozen moments, bottled scents and a series of montages behind a glass window, on display for me to visit, again and again.

CHAPTER 4

SWIMMING WITH CROCODILES

The grown-ups are determined to keep calm and carry on as normal. As the war grows more intense, so does their zest for life. "Everyone must have a bloody good time, don't let the war dampen your spirits."

The local Country Club is the epicentre of the 'jolly good time'. Golf, cricket, tennis, lawn bowls, gentlemen-only bars, Whites-only membership and cocktail hour have been exported to the British colonies to provide an oasis of cultural imperialism in primitive Africa.

The Country Club is more than a local drinking hole and sports facility. It emulates the lifestyle of the British aristocracy, whose sporting activities like polo, fox hunting and lawn tennis took place on lavish country estates. Rhodesians evolved into a plucky hybrid of British elitism, folded in on itself and baked in the sun, believing their culture to be superior and more sophisticated, arrogantly assuming that the Africans had no culture of their own.

Trying to maintain the finer traditions of the English genteel in Africa is no easy task. The heat alone can beat any class out of you. In Africa, jam and cream scones slump into a mush of curdled cream and floundering flies. Cucumber sandwiches go limp, shrivel and turn crusty. Procedure and bureaucracy blister in the sun, while slouched human shapes sit under pointless shade with vacant eyes, indifferent to an obsession with efficiency.

On the days we go with Dad to the club, we know we could be there long into the night. After golf, tennis or bowls, everyone heads to the 19th hole, the bar. No kids allowed. We roam around the club grounds, playing our own games and while we grow tired and hungry, the grown-ups grow more raucous in the pub.

The club smells of Cobra polish, spilt beer and stale smoke. Children must go to the back door of the pub where the African waiters collect trays of drinks. We try and get Dad's attention, hoping we can get a Coke or a plate of hot chips.

We have blankets and pillows in the car and can put ourselves to bed when we are worn out and chilled from the frost that coats the grass. It's a place to forget, to barricade from the unrelenting stress of the war with booze and joviality. Drinking is a national pastime.

Most holidays we set off for Kariba, the largest man-made lake in the world. We join a throng of families to waterski, fish, sunbathe, and camp at the lakeside resort, Caribbea Bay. According to Mom, we have packed everything except the kitchen sink!

It is extremely dangerous to travel on open roads during the guerrilla bush war. Ambushes and landmines are a regular occurrence. This does not stop us. Instead, we team up with other families and travel in convoy with armed escorts. We put our lives in the hands of the minesweepers who patrol the roads and hope they haven't missed any.

No one stops to ask if this is bravery, madness or stupidity. Perhaps it is admirable, in the same way one admires those who swim with sharks, dive off cliffs or wrestle crocodiles. The difference is these die-hard adventurers have packed guns and a picnic and are taking their wives and kids along for the ride.

The convoy forms a long snake of cars, caravans, trailers and boats filled with camping and fishing gear. At the head and tail of the snake are the army vehicles, followed by the men with guns and cold beers. The belly of the snake bulges with women, children and bags of oranges and sarmies. The air is electric with nervous excitement.

In anticipation of both the holiday and the possibility of an ambush, our little eyes peer over the windows, squinting at the grass and trees for signs of Terrs. Dad says, "There will be absolutely NO pit stops, NO wees in the bushes, no stopping under ANY circumstances. We do not want to be sitting ducks."

The men are tense but full of bravado with beers and guns pointing out the windows. The moms keep their hands on the steering wheel, knuckles white, dishing out sweets and smacks. We are told, "Keep your head down or it will get shot off!"

We try to build pillow barricades and claim our back seat territory. My sister and I fight, kicking, pinching and pushing. Our bickering eventually has our mom threatening to give us a bloody hiding, her arm flaying around the back of the car trying to give us a 'klap'.

The chatting of the moms stops, and it is dead quiet as we begin to descend a narrow road on the escarpment to Kariba town. The vehicles sway under their bulging loads. Petrol restrictions require sharing cars, and all our luggage is on someone else's boat, safely under a tarpaulin. I look up at the steep, scrubby hills surrounding us, feeling watched and a lot like a sitting duck.

One crack of a bullet or the glint of metal from the bush and we know what to do. No nagging, no back chat, no smacks needed. Crawl behind the seat of the car and cover your head.

"Are we there yet?"

Finally, we arrive, dishevelled and eyes dry from unblinking, wide-eyed watchfulness and a bit disappointed that we did not see a Terr get shot.

Our summer holiday stretches out like a long waking yawn.

Inside the resort the children roam around in mismatched gangs, bonded together, away from the camping families. The perimeter of the resort is heavily guarded and patrolled but this is kept well hidden, so we can all relax. We all need a break from the war.

Caribbea Bay Resort is everything a 1970's summer resort should be – a perfect blend of kitsch and cool. It is a poor man's paradise with every holiday cliché on the banks of a lake as large as a small sea. Caribbean-style white chalets cluster along cobbled paths. Thatched poolside bars serve cocktails with paper umbrellas. Bronzed ladies smothered in baby oil lie on pool loungers. One of the pools has a fake rocky waterfall feature and another pool has a round island tiled with a bright orange crab.

At night, coloured lights dance along the promenade leading to the open-air-disco dance floor with a mirror ball fracturing its light. We love to watch everyone boogie to Abba and The Bee Gees, all dressed up in bell bottoms and halter-neck dresses, tie-dyed caftans and miniskirts. Mom has silver stilettos but she's taller than Dad so she can only wear them if Dad wears his platforms. Dad's a good dancer and he lets us stand on his feet and waltz around.

Camping life is relaxed and free of school time routines and bedtime curfews. Instead, there are endless days of swimming and fishing, braais and picnics. The days are warm and grassy and are spent swimming in the lake under the wooden jetty or in one of the three swimming pools.

In the evening, grey clouds of gnats float out of the long grass, filling the air like a plague, vanishing miraculously as the dew forms a damp carpet. Mosquitos emerge as the night air sinks, heavy and warm. Moths, beetles, stink bugs and stick insects swarm the campsite lamps like night pilgrims to a holy bright temple. Night sounds hum and chirrup and the water reeds choke with croaking frogs.

Our shrieks and shouts cut through the air as we play hide-and-seek, stuck-in-the-mud and cricket until we can't see our hands in front of our faces. We skulk back to the shadows of our tents and burrow into sleeping bags. I drift off to sleep, listening to the adults talking loudly and laughing raucously till they too eventually stumble to bed. Sleep comes quickly and I dream of crocodiles and razor-toothed tigerfish, of green water and silky weeds grasping my ankles.

We wake up with the sun, bright and shining with promise. We are going to spend the day on the lake in Uncle Bert's fishing boat. Uncle Bert is not an actual uncle. The boat is called 'Hairy Legs'. It is my childhood nickname. Dad and Uncle Bert call everyone 'Hairy Legs'. Except for each other. They call each other Bert-a-rino and Wither-rino.

We chug out into the water in the coolness and quietness of the morning. The boat is sluggish, laden with two families, fishing gear and a day's supply of beer in the cooler box. There is also vino for the ladies and a selection of sarmies wrapped in tin foil. They will be warm by the time we eat them. There are large sticks of salty, spicy biltong – dried game meat. When still tender, we can chew on it like teething toddlers. If the meat strips are dry, we can tear papery pieces off with our teeth. I can eat it till my jaws ache.

We have all been allowed to go on the day trip if we don't interfere with the men's activities. Fishing, drinking beer and badgering each other. It's not practical for us all to stay on the boat so the women and children will be left at a picnic spot while the men fish.

Our first drop-off site is a small alcove near the Sinyati Gorge. Every time we come here, Dad reminds us that he wants his ashes scattered in the gorge. The small beach crunches with coarse sand and there is a long shallow shelf of water, a lucid pale green. The water dips off the shelf into a dark, blind green. The deepest parts of the lake plunge to depths of 97 metres.

Dad says the crocs prefer deeper water so we should be okay in the shallow part, but we should also avoid anything looking like a floating log. I think of the poem I learnt at school about a lonely croc lying all day on a sunny rock. I check for sunny rocks and lonely crocs just in case Dad has forgotten crocs also like the sun.

The beach is at the bottom of a deep ravine. Rocky cliffs rise sharply around us like crooked skyscrapers, the tops merge with the blinding sunlight and vanish out of sight. From time to time, the haunting, soulful cry of a fish eagle echoes through the gorge. It is the mournful song of Africa, and it gives me goosebumps. The cliffs are too dense and steep for the terrorists, so we aren't sitting ducks.

Dad and Uncle Bert speed off to hunt for tigerfish, sought-after game fish with razor-sharp teeth and a whole lot of fight in them. Tigerfish look like hyenas with scales and fins, their heads and terrifying teeth attached to a scaly body. Conical, dog-like teeth designed to intermesh. They attack their prey, disembowelling and shredding it in multiple charges. Prized catches are stuffed and mounted, their teeth open like gin traps, lest you forget you could lose your hand trying to land one of these ferocious water monsters. They are standard décor in any Rhodesian home bar.

We are sunburnt castaways by the time the boat fetches us. We go in search of Hippo Island. The island is a unique mass of gigantic rock formations with dead trees rooted in their crevices. It is otherworldly, like a floating Stonehenge. In the water, blackened branches of dead trees reach up to the heavens like souls trapped in watery graves. It gives me the heebie-jeebies. We are allowed a quick dip in the water, but we must jump in and out and not swim around too much. The water is deep and dark, so we clamber on the rocks and take quick adrenaline-fuelled dips in the spooky water. We squeal when something touches our limbs. They are the same giddy squeals of happy terror we make when Dad pretends to be the Boogeyman. Years later, we learn small planes flying over Kariba see huge dark shapes swimming around the island.

We should be heading back as it is getting late, it is not a good idea to be on the lake after dark. We have drifted off course and we can see the Zambian border in the distance. This is enemy territory and a crossing point for guerrillas to enter Rhodesia. It is patrolled by Zambian police who are friendly with the terrorists and not so friendly with us. The moms are anxious, the kids are tired and crabby. The men, intoxicated from fishing conquests and beer, are throwing caution to the wind.

Dad says, "We are out of shooting range and muntus can't swim. Anyway, the crocs will get them first." Why will the crocs eat them and not us, I wonder? Dad's rules can be puzzling but I guess he knows best so we should be safe. Even so, I watch the green underbrush of the coast carefully as we float closer to the island.

We glide into a grassy bay with shady flat trees. The water pools into the bay from long sandy channels flanked with tall grass. It is unlike the other places we have been to, a deathly still beauty. Untouched and whispering its own ancient secrets. It whispers of the two-toed tribe that once lived on the land, now buried deep below the man-made dam. They are sometimes called the Ostrich People of Zimbabwe, a rare genetic mutation called Lobster-claw Syndrome gives them their strange two-toed feet. They worship the river god, Nyaminyami, who some say has the body of a snake and the head of a fish. His image is now sold as cheap carved souvenirs and walking sticks to tourists. The water is glass, golden yellow with dappled sunshine. Shoals of silvery Kapenta reflect the light coming through the trees in fleeting flashes. These fish, the size of my pinkie finger, are used for bait or dried and salted to be sold by the Africans as a snack. We swim silently in the warm water, careful not to stick our heads up out of the grass. We don't want to get our mugs shot off.

The sun sinks, a red globe turning all the silhouettes black, the water is flat and still. Everyone is quiet and I am filled with love and fear that sticks in my throat. I love this land with fierce pride and devotion. I do not yet understand the cost of loving something that can never love me back. I do not yet know I sing my war songs for a lost, doomed and morally bankrupt cause. I don't know that the monsters I call 'terrorists' call themselves 'Freedom Fighters'.

They are fighting for liberation and freedom. We are fighting to keep White rule in Rhodesia and the communists out. We are supposed to be a shining beacon of hope in darkest Africa, filled with rampant corruption, violent dictators, disease, famine and a myriad of other problems. We are trying to do what is best for the Africans. But since we are White colonialists, we are not exactly to be trusted. Our ancestors took this land with violence and bloodshed, bribing local chiefs with battery-operated radios and other worthless tokens of wealth, trinkets traded for vast tracts of land or mining rights. Like cheap Christmas cracker charms, which break, leaving only the sound of the crack, a hiss of smoke and a slightly foul smell after the cracker is pulled.

So, now we wear our 'Rhodesia is Super' T-shirts and sing our songs. We send our men and boys to fight for what we believe in with all our hearts, that the Whites should always be in charge, otherwise everything will go to the dogs. Everyone, including our dad, must do their part, keep watch, go on call-ups, travel in convoys, be part of the civilian reserves so we can all maintain a strangely twisted version of normal.

It's not normal.

These are the remnants of my childhood, tinged with a kind of madness. I find myself grasping and clutching to moments of purity and bliss in mayhem, trying to find something to hold onto before it disintegrates and crumbles to ashes.

The history that has formed me and shaped me has been evaluated, sifted, rejected, discarded, dismantled and stripped away. It is a White man's fable, twisted and bent by those who wrote the history books. The wicked and the noble, the civilised and the savage. The victims and perpetrators are characters chosen by the authors of history and written in black and white. Black Savage. White Explorer. Black Victim. White Perpetrator. Black Terrorist. White Soldier. Patriot. Communist. Now the terrorist, Mugabe, is the president. The White president is a traitor.

Everything is grey. Dust and ashes.

Still, rescued from those ruins are those shining moments of bubbling laughter, of swimming till the sun has vanished, of ice-cold Coke from a glass bottle and salty Willards crisps, of freewheeling down a dusty road with watering eyes.

CHAPTER 5

THE CHICKEN RUN

We are doing the Chicken Run. This land is no longer our land, even though we have fought through 'thick and thin'. We are emigrating to South Africa. We are called 'chickens' by those who stay behind because we are afraid of Black rule, and we are traitors because we are giving up and leaving. The Whites that emigrate retort, "Turn the lights off when you leave."

We have sung our patriotic war songs and said our prayers but no amount of singing and praying has prevented the inevitable. We have lost The War.

My parents are teachers and Dad says that he wants a better life for us all and that things will be going downhill from now on. What he really means is he doesn't want us being educated with Blacks at school. I hear the adults say, "The problem is, ten-year-old kids will be in class with bladdy seventeen-year-old munts who can barely read and write. The bladdy terrorists are bloody war heroes now! They will bring them to the schools in bus loads."

I try to picture myself squashed next to a much older Black boy in the classroom. Will there really be Terrs at my school? Ever since

I can remember we have had bomb and terrorist attack drills at school, crouching under our desks with our hands over our heads in case the Terrs come. Now they are apparently coming in bus loads. And they will be sitting at our desks next to us. What if a big Black boy tries to kiss me with his African lips? Takkie lips. Like the thick ridged soles of my Bata takkies. African lips like the ones the terrorists cut off and made people eat. I have never kissed a boy. Not a proper kiss anyway. I've seen the teenagers kissing in the back of cars at the rundown drive-in. It looks disgusting, like they are sucking on each other's faces.

So now we are leaving. I have to say goodbye to everything and everyone I know. How do I say goodbye to a country? How do I say goodbye to the narrow, worn footpaths that furrow through long grass, the mulberries that stain my lips and feet, the lucky beans I keep in my pockets, the places and things as familiar to me as my own chewed fingernails? The smell of rain hitting dry dirt, the bamboo trees that whisper my secrets back to me, and my friend who I love like my sister?

We pack up everything we can take with us and sell the rest. We are going 'down south'. At least it is still run by Whites, they are Afrikaners, but they will have to do. We are English Whites. They are 'Boers', far less refined with their thick accents and blatant hatred for Black people. Ours is more subtle. Apartheid is just a foreign Afrikaans word. Afrikaans is a new language I am forced to learn. I will grow to hate it because it will drag my mark average down.

The new government has placed restrictions on the amount of cash you can take out the country. Dad has already taken Gladness, our maid, on two 'holidays' to South Africa. Gladness has not really gone on a holiday. Dad has taken her with him on two trips to South Africa just so he can use her holiday allowance to get some extra cash out of the country.

We leave the little town of Chinhoyi and move in with my Aunty Jane and our cousins in Harare, while Dad goes ahead to South Africa to start a job and get everything ready for our family to move. He is going to sell carpets for 3M Company.

I am to attend my cousin's school for one term. I am eleven years old and I will move schools another five times before I turn thirteen. This is the beginning of my unravelling. I will, from this moment on, feel like I am swimming with dislocated limbs, flailing about with my head barely above water. My feet never quite reach the ground again and like the first time I am dumped by a wave, I lose all sense of where I am, my nose and eyes burn, my mouth is full of sand.

Something in me has loosened. It seems like a small shift, barely perceptible, like a twig that breaks, falls and starts an avalanche. This is the moment something snaps. I've lost my anchoring and am drifting. Soon my good manners and school achievements will be a paper-thin wall, hiding loss, grief and insecurity. No one will notice I am drowning. No one will come to my rescue.

※

Dad comes back to Rhodesia – we refuse to call it by its new name 'Zimbabwe' – to fetch us a few months later. He was supposed to find us a house first, but he misses his family, so he gets into his car one day and drives all day and night to fetch us. This was not the plan.

We load everything we own into our car and Sprite caravan and set off on the Chicken Run. We laugh at how we look like real Africans with all our belongings piled up. We are moving to Umhlanga, the French riviera of South Africa. We will live a block away from the exotic Cabana Beach resort in a caravan park. Homeless, living like poor Whites in a trailer park. Immigrants. Starting from scratch. Gladness will not be coming with us this time.

In Chinhoyi, I have been king of the anthill. In South Africa, I am an ant at the foot of a mountain. My little country town has not prepared me for the sophistication and complexities of being twelve in a modern city like Durban. I miss the social cues, wear the wrong clothes, my games are childish. I feel like a square peg trying to fit into a round hole. We are called 'When-we's'. "When we were in Rhodesia ..." Apparently South Africans don't think Rhodesia is super. It's not long before I stop telling people where I come from.

It's mortifying to tell anyone I live in a caravan park. I don't invite any friends over. It's three months before we move to a little house with a blue door and concrete garden walls, but we land up still camping in the house because we don't have any furniture. We sit in the lounge on grubby deck chairs and sleep on the floor on camping mattresses and sleeping bags. It's worse than the campsite because we can't pretend we are just on holiday.

I never thought about being rich or poor before. I think we must be poor now. I never knew half the things we can't afford even existed. I didn't know knickerbockers and luminous cut-off tops were this summer must-haves. I didn't know about being cool. I didn't know you needed boot-style lace-up skates to keep up with the kids playing on the street. I didn't know the girls my age don't wear homemade clothes or dresses that match their eight-year-old sister's. I want to go back to the place where knickerbockers and fancy skates don't matter. I want to go back to my anthill. I want to go back to locusts catapulting out of knee-high grass. I want to go back to being bossy on the playground. I want to go back to making up dances to *Grease* and Abba. I want to go back to the fears I am familiar with and the hiding places I can find in the dark. I want to go back.

I do believe my parents love me unconditionally. I have just never really put it to the test. I am a super-achiever. On the little anthill, I was almost always the best at everything. Top of the class, lead in the school plays, victrix ludorum in both athletics and swimming. First team of any sport I played. I was a champion. My parents were obviously proud of me, but I never gave them any reason not to be. Teachers' kids were under scrutiny, and I never let them down.

I have certificates, awards, ribbons and trophies for being top of the anthill, always expecting no less than my absolute best. It is easy to underestimate me and not see the fiercely competitive and determined 'win at all costs' spirit contained in my waif-like body. My greatest victory was winning the cross-country races by a full lap of the field, leaving everyone behind in the dust, including all the boys, whose faces were red with sweat and humiliation. My dad was a champion, a sports hero with albums full of newspaper clippings. He played hockey for Rhodesia against South Africa, Australia, Germany and New Zealand. I liked to make him proud of me.

But here in South Africa, I am just the new girl. It's almost the end of Grade Six. I'll have one year left to prove myself and find my place in this new world.

I have no track record, no one is nervous to swim or run against me. I am nobody. The cross-country race is a few weeks away and the school is buzzing with talk of the rivalry between the two top runners in the school. One girl is already on the South African junior athletic squad, the other girl is the only one with a chance to beat her over a longer distance. Nobody knows I have decided to win the race. I keep quiet as a country mouse, the bigger the surprise of an outsider winning, the sweeter the victory will be.

On the day of the race, I put on my trusty old Bata takkies. I have become convincing at explaining why I prefer Bata to trendy

Adidas. I am even able to explain why my ancient second-hand strap-on roller skates are better for speed and doing tricks than the latest rollerblades. I've convinced myself I don't want new ones.

I have a strategy and as the gun goes off for the race, I know I will rather die than come second or third. I have this one single moment to become somebody. One opportunity to stop being invisible. One chance to feel like I belong.

I start at a good pace and keep the leaders in sight. I know the exact moment I will overtake them. I wait until I am five hundred metres from the steep uphill stretching for two kilometres to the summit of this monumental climb, almost out of sight. I change gears to a pace just short of a sprint and start to charge up the hill. I must have passed them, but all I see is the scrubby uneven dirt trail in front of each stride.

I was born to run on terrain like this. It is two full blocks of undeveloped land on the left side of the school. It's grassy, bumpy, uneven and I've sprinted through bush like this my whole life. Everything falls away and it's just me and this hill. All I can hear is my rasping breath and every thud of my Bata takkies hitting the ground. My chest is burning. My heart feels like a jackhammer pounding in my chest.

At some point I stop feeling the scream of my muscles. It's just me thundering up the hill with every ounce of grit and determination I can muster. I start to feel like I am floating, weightless and light. The whole universe has stopped for this one moment and everything else fades away as my long, lanky legs carry me to the top.

I run along the last stretch of road and back down to the school in a blur, bursting onto the field for the finishing lap. I am alone on the track, and I hear gasps and murmurs from the crowd. I am in full sprint now, flushed with adrenaline and exhilaration.

I could run forever and ever. I win. The outsider, the dark horse, the new girl.

I wait eagerly to be celebrated but instead, everyone is wondering where the favourites are. The race is more about which of the two favourites will win second and third place. My fleeting moment of glory fizzles out while I slump to the ground, exhausted.

I wait for school on Monday for accolades and my place to move up in the pecking order, but my win is considered a fluke, a one-hit wonder and somehow an insult to the two other runners. I humiliated them and yet I am the one feeling defeated and confused. I've never felt bad about winning before. It is the only social strategy I know, and it's failed dismally.

CHAPTER 6

DROWNING

I begin my first year of high school at Danville Park Girls and will be here for two school terms. Mom and Dad have started new jobs at a private boys' school on the other side of town. My little sisters have gone with, and I am left with the neighbours until I can move schools again. My folks have dragged the caravan round the block and parked it in the garden of a family of ex-Rhodesians. I sleep in the caravan and eat meals with the host family.

Halfway through the year, I am offered a scholarship to attend Durban Girls' College, the sister school of Clifton Boys' Preparatory where my family now live. My parents are over the moon because I will be getting a top-notch education at one of the most prestigious private schools in South Africa. This is what they have sacrificed everything for.

I am not thrilled. I feel exhausted. I am tired of scratchy new uniforms and looking for someone to sit next to. New girl shame. I can't shut out the drowning, underwater sensation and dread that fills me.

There are no terrorists at the window, the dangers are shifting shadows and shapeless figures I strain to see. My dreams are filled with silent screams throttled and gurgling in my throat and legs of lead sucked into the ground making it impossible to run. I dream of currents dragging me out to sea and every time I come up for air, I gulp in water but something grabs my limbs, pulling me back down into black water. I keep swimming, I keep running and screaming and wake up in a damp sweat. I fight and pound at the water, grabbing and grasping to find something to hold on to.

I am tenacious and iron-willed. I work hard to keep up, in a place of academic excellence. A is average and B is mediocre. I stare out the windows, scribble and doodle on my lever arch files. I hate Maths, it never adds up for me. Mrs Lemcool, my Math teacher, and I come to an unspoken agreement. We will ignore each other. I try out for sports teams, the drama club and hedge around tightly knit social groups. Most of the girls have been here since Grade One. They have had a seven-year head start on their friendships and cliques. Seven years of playdates and sleepovers.

I make one friend. She is a tall, goofy redhead and is crazy about the frozen cheese sandwiches my mom packs me for school lunches. Mom gets our maid to make them a week ahead and wrap them in tin foil. I am good at being the third wheel, the second-best friend and the tag-along. I am used to being on the fringes.

When my final year of school is finished, I will have many friends but no deep attachments, no unbreakable bonds. I am fiercely independent, self-reliant. I have fashioned my own weapons of survival.

While my hormones are raging, forming zits, teenage angst and mood swings, something else has taken shape deep in my subconscious. It starts to rise, gaining momentum, bubbling beneath the surface.

The girl I see in the mirror is gawky, skinny, uncomfortable in her body and often withdrawn. Beyond the reflection, below the skin, behind the dark brown eyes, something is growing, seething and heaving. It's pushing back as if there's a little beat-up kid inside me desperate to stand up to the bully. Finally, with bruised arms and scraped knees, the scrappy, gritty little me gets up and hurls herself at everything pushing her down and kicking her in the guts. Invisibility and insignificance.

Growing like a fire in my belly is a war cry. Outrage. It screams "I will not be insignificant! I will not be invisible! I will not go unnoticed!" This primal hunger to be seen and heard gives birth to the class clown, the freak show, the punk, the rebel.

Truth or dare? Dare every single time. I discover other ways to get attention and I lap them up hungrily. If I can't fit in, I will stand out. This is liberating. I don't have to care my mom drives an ancient Datsun 500 so rusted you can see the road through the floorboards. It looks like a stray dog next to the sleek Jaguars and Mercedes-Benzes rolling up to collect the daughters of doctors, lawyers, businessmen and diplomats. I don't care we can't afford to shop at the fashion boutiques at Musgrave Centre. I wear my school uniform at the mall after school. It's a bloody green and white status symbol! I cut my hair into a punk rock buzz cut with a tail at the back and spikes in the front. I am promptly suspended.

I develop a strangely androgynous fashion style, part New Romantic, borderline homeless. I raid my Dad's closet for oversized jackets and collared shirts. I wear his ties with white vests and braces. I always wear Bata takkies. Being different is my crusade, shock tactics are my secret weapon and bitter insecurities are stuffed down as deep as I can swallow them, buried beneath spunky bravado.

Art is my refuge, the place I am always able to find roots. It is the place I feel truly at home in my own skin. It's the one remaining place I can still outshine others, thanks to an art teacher who looks for more than good copycat skills. I spend most of the class restless, sharpening my pencil, pacing up and down and often leave to draw outside. I like drawing with black ink. I like committing black ink to paper with no margin for error. It's hardcore. In the last fifteen minutes of the class, I scribble furiously with my black pen. I try to scratch beneath the subject's skin to fashion something of its essence and character. Painstaking reproduction of the subject bores me to tears and I lack the focus for it. The hours I spent as a child watching my father paint watercolour landscapes taught me a language of brushstrokes, and hatched lines are my mother tongue.

※

The rest of my high school years are filled with the usual schoolgirl antics that we will reminisce about one day, sipping on champagne at posh school reunions. I have my first kiss at my sixteenth birthday party with a tall Jewish boy named David. He tastes like a wet ashtray and my dad ends the party by switching the hall lights on at 9pm, telling everyone to "bugger off".

I don't want to know about politics, unrest, violence, apartheid or sanctions. I want to shut all those uncomfortable realities out, ignore them and listen to Duran Duran, Sade and David Bowie on my Walkman. The highlight of my week is Popshop on Fridays at 6pm so I can record my favourite music videos on our VHS. 'Video killed the radio star.' Dad is livid when I accidentally tape over *Cry of the Kalahari*. He has now decided the Kalahari Bushmen are the only true inhabitants of Africa. He hates Popshop.

I care about my suntan and getting a body like Jane Fonda, doing aerobics and jumping around in a leotard and leg warmers. I want to know who shot JR Ewing on the TV drama *Dallas*. We are all glued to our TVs every Tuesday at 8pm to watch the latest antics of the Ewing oil empire. We live under a mushroom cloud of nuclear anxiety. The end of the world is a touch of a button away. We are all at the mercy of the Heads of the USSR and the USA, praying that they will not lose their own heads and get trigger happy.

Alphaville sings "Forever Young" – "Hoping for the best, but expecting the worst, are you gonna drop the bomb or not?" – but I am used to living under heavy shadows and dark foreboding clouds. We were supposed to leave terrorism, violence and the war behind us for Pete's sake. We moved on.

We are here in South Africa for a fresh start. We are politically fatigued. It's unspeakably easy to be ignorant and live in our White suburban utopia. We are fed the same diet of propaganda and lies I grew up on. All the dirty secrets swept under rugs and townships far out of sight. We sometimes feel pity for all of those less fortunate. Our school gives generously to the Feed the Babies Fund.

CHAPTER 7

DEFLOWERED

I am a late bloomer. I'm seventeen and a half and still a virgin. I haven't had a serious boyfriend yet. I have made up my mind. I will not lose my virginity to a pimple-faced, clumsy, groping boy. I am keeping myself for a real man who knows something about seduction.

I'm not a swan but I'm no longer an ugly duckling either. My lanky legs with knobbly knees are now long and slender. Curves have filled out, softening my gawky edges. I am pear-shaped but it's a juicy pear, my voluptuous butt and tiny waist are not at all like the narrow-hipped boyish body type of the supermodels like Cindy Crawford and Naomi Campbell. I am starting to notice that my long legs and my curves turn heads. My hair has grown out into a wild black 80's permed mane. What's more, I have found a man to deflower me.

When Mom and Dad tell me that they are moving to teach at Cordwalles in Pietermaritzburg shortly before my final year, I refuse to move schools. There is no way in hell I am starting over again.

Anyway, they know it's better academically for me to stay and finish my matric in Durban. I stay at school as a boarder during the week and catch the Greyhound home on the weekends. The boarding house girls are mostly farmers' daughters. They are down to earth, raucous and we feast on copious piles of toast in our common room and laugh till we pee our pants. I love everything about being a boarder – the overcooked food, the lumpy mattress, the loopy matron who no longer scares us, the musty furniture and the perpetual smell of polish and floor cleaner. Most of all I love my brief year with this girl gang.

On the weekends I tell Mom I'll be studying for my final exams by the Cordwalles school pool. I take my files and head across the fields to the pool at the far end of the school ground. It's a smaller school campus than Sinoia High but full of preppy school charm and traditions upholding generations of privilege. We live in a charming teacher's cottage down a little gravel road at the back of the school. I've noticed I may be being watched by male eyes while languishing at the pool in my bikini. I stare blankly at the biology file, never turning the pages. I feel the warmth of the sun and a deeper kind of heat on my body. I've been noticed. I like being spied on.

There are several attractive young men, varsity students who are in residence at the school in exchange for assisting with sports coaching and school duties. I have seen them around a few times. There are four boarder masters. To me, they are men, not boys.

Seth is one of the boarder masters. He is two years older than me and in his second year of law. I've bumped into Seth a few times. He gets along well with Dad. When I see him my heart races and I panic, worried I'm going to say or do something stupid. I aim for aloof and mysterious. It's ridiculous to think he would be interested in a schoolgirl like me. He tells me the schoolboys watch me swimming from the dining hall window and they say, "Mr Wither's daughter is hot." I feel a flush of pleasure.

Seth has scraggly long blond hair, broad shoulders and a mischievous twinkle in his blue eyes. He teases me without saying a word. I think he's flirting with me, but I am not sure I am reading the signs correctly. Act cool.

He's agreed to be my date for our school leavers' dinner. It's our final night on the town after exams. It's our own end-of-year party and not the stuffy awkward school hall dance. This is a 'let your hair down', 'go wild' night.

I'm wearing a nude pink ballet tutu with a strapless boob tube top. I'm bronzed after many hours lying by the pool. Seth picks me up in his red truck. It has a white canopy and a foam mattress in the back. I am dizzy, almost intoxicated and breathless, sitting so close to him in the car and dancing with him in the hotel banquet hall. After the party we go for a walk on the beach promenade. I keep telling myself he's here out of politeness or obligation. Maybe it would be rude to turn down Mr Wither's daughter. My mother says he looks like trouble. She knows he is devilishly charming; his cheeky grin doesn't fool her.

We sit on the edge of the pier, our legs dangle over the edge of the midnight sea and the warm sea breeze makes my skirt flutter. He leans closer and I feel his warm breath on my neck as he whispers, "I want to kiss you." The crashing waves drown out the sound of my thumping heart and I think I may melt when his lips touch mine.

Too tired and drunk to drive an hour back to Pietermaritzburg, we look for a place to stay the night. Seth ramps his truck over the pavement, misses a few trees, the swings and a merry-go-round, and stops in the middle of Bulwer Park. How convenient, there's a mattress in the back of the truck. But he just curls up and sleeps very respectfully next to me.

If you had driven past the park the following Sunday morning or walked your dog there, you would have seen a dishevelled girl in a crumpled tutu climb out of a truck and walk barefoot down to the edge of the park, on her way to get a drink of water from the drinking fountain. However, you would probably not have been able to see that this young girl would soon fall deeply in love with the man in the truck, believing that she'd found the man that she would want to give every part of herself to, that she would trust him with the sacred rite of passage from girl to woman, that he would deflower her. And that he would break her heart.

There are many opportunities for him to seduce her. There are camping and water-skiing weekends at Midmar Dam, there are times he takes her to his parents' house and they fall asleep in his bedroom.

He is always a gentleman. It's infuriating. He calls me 'Frenchie'. I love that. He says I remind him of a Parisian girl, someone exotic. When I look in the mirror, I begin to see a different girl. A blossoming orchid unfurling in a moist dark greenhouse. I see sultry dark eyes heavily lined in black kohl. I see my prominent cheekbones and heart-shaped lips. I see my olive skin and someone who exudes sensuality.

I've realised something about myself. It will profoundly change me. I am not pretty. I am not cute. I am not beautiful. There is something about me, not skin deep, it is more powerful and dangerous. It's a weapon. I will learn to wield it with skill and ruthless accuracy. I am sexy and my awareness of the effect I can have on men is fascinating to me. I have discovered a whole new way to stop being invisible. Mixing this newly discovered sensuality with my need to be noticed, to shock and be outrageous, is like dousing a fire with gasoline. A ticking bomb. Boom.

Seth does not want to make love to me. He understands something I have yet to grasp. He knows sex changes everything and creates a bond not easily broken. He does not want a bond with me. I don't understand why he pulls away.

But now he doesn't have a choice as I've diarised January 1st, 1987 as the day I will sleep with him. We are drunk enough but not too drunk. Just enough for all resolve and reason to have been drowned out by desire. His bedroom lamp has a red bulb bathing his studio flat with fire. The soundtrack playing is Rodriguez. 'I wonder', 'Sugarman' and 'Crucify your mind' lure me into a seduction trance.

※

Sometimes, I wonder what would have happened if I had let an inexperienced boy fumble his way through my first time. What if it had been a humiliating mess, lasting a few forgettable moments on the back seat of a parked car? What if it had been awkward and awful and meaningless? What if my heart was absent that day, busy with other engagements and unavailable? What if I wasn't already falling in love?

Seth will later regret crossing a boundary that binds us together. From now on, he will pull back and then be drawn towards me in a never-ending cycle of desire and desperate fear of being hurt again. He has acted against his better judgement.

It is too late when I find out that he was in a long relationship with a girl who cheated on him. I find a shoebox full of love letters and photographs in his sock drawer. He has sealed up his heart in the crumpled box and put it far away. I hated her.

He has told me, "You don't want to be tied down with me in your first year at varsity. You need to have fun, go out with lots of guys. They'll be all over you! You'll forget about me when all those first-year guys are around."

He tries to tease me and be light-hearted, but I feel him pushing me away. I pout and sulk playfully, hiding the hurt and rejection. I am just a mistake to him, something to regret and get over. He wants me to move on.

I have zero emotional intelligence and lash out with the bluntest tool I can find. Make him jealous. I flirt shamelessly with his friends. Then I kiss them. Then I eventually sleep with one of them, driving the betrayal dagger as deep as I can, destroying the trust of the only person I want more than anyone else.

CHAPTER 8

REBEL, REBEL

I am noticeable on the Pietermaritzburg campus. I am loud, act promiscuously and love every bit of attention I am getting. I dance on tables and behave badly, whether I am drunk or sober. I love it when the guys turn to look twice as I strut past. I have fine-tuned the ability to turn heads when I enter a room. Every outfit I wear is chosen to attract attention. Being an art student is a permission slip for self-expression. My look is sporty slut meets tacky cowgirl. I wear knee high boots with fringes down the sides, they flick around my legs when I flounce around campus.

My favourite outfit is wearing Dad's rugby socks with my Bata takkies and men's rugby shorts. I have damn fine legs. I soon hear my nickname is Puss in Boots. I love it. I play up to it and feed it. Here kitty kitty. I do not blend in anywhere. I don't give a rat's arse. I definitely don't blend in at 'Hippie Ville', the art department. Art students waft around in tie-dye caftans and leather sandals, smoking pot and being philosophical. I loathe the pompous art lecturers who make up academic bullshit and have obvious favourites. I don't think I am cut out to be a true artist, I just can't buy into the academic pontificating. I decide to switch to drama in my second year.

My parents boot me out of home and move me into a flat near campus before I turn 18. I have become intolerable, impossibly defiant and an embarrassment. I can't speak to my dad without it becoming a shouting match.

He yells, "You can't go out dressed like that!"

"I can and I will."

"Okay, then just don't bloody well go anywhere near the school!"

Respectable teachers can't have a daughter like me parading about in front of the snooty mommies and daddies dropping their darlings off at school.

There are several things one shouldn't do if your parents teach at a posh school. You shouldn't be in a boarder master's bedroom on a Monday morning when you are woken by your father's voice doing the early morning school duty, waking up sleepy young boys in their dormitories for breakfast. You shouldn't still be wearing the dress you had on the night before at the fundraising school function you went to with all the staff, parents and boarder masters. You should not get drunk at school functions. You shouldn't try to sneak out of Seth's bedroom as the school bell clangs. You really shouldn't try to get across the school courtyard, past the headmaster and secretaries' office, carrying your stilettos, still wearing a ballgown and with your hair unbrushed. You shouldn't be seen running around the back of your mom's Grade One classroom, dashing across the field like a slutty Cinderella.

You shouldn't go skinny dipping alone with all the boarder masters in the school pool on a Saturday night. You shouldn't drag a mattress down to the school's audio-visual room so you can watch pornography with your on-again off-again boyfriend. You should not have sex on the floor of the audio room where young minds listen to David

Attenborough narrate the mating rituals of the praying mantis.

You shouldn't sneak out in the night to spy on Seth when he goes out on another date. You shouldn't break into the school chapel and climb into the bell tower facing his room on the opposite side of the grass garden. You shouldn't look for the shadow of another girl against the red light in the window. You shouldn't let your heart get broken, turning you into an obsessive, stalking, sobbing maniac. You shouldn't retaliate by making sure the door is slightly ajar so Seth can see you naked in the bed with pretty boy Sean, his friend. You shouldn't betray and crush the only person you care about. You shouldn't do something so self-destructive, making you feel like trash, riddling you with regret and destroying any chance of him trusting you. Ever.

✦

So, I am officially out of the nest, out of sight and living in my own little flat with another art student. There's no need to sneak around now. I am unchained and fully committed to a path of self-destruction. Hungry for all the wrong kinds of validation, waving my tattered reputation in defiance like a soiled flag. Truth or dare? Dare every time.

I relish shocking the stuck up, tight-arsed judgemental bitches who hiss and whisper behind my back. I couldn't care less what they think of me. Watch your boyfriends, girls, there's a Man-eater on the prowl. I kissed nine of them at one party. I see the look in their eyes glazed with beer and desire and I feed on it, eating them alive, licking a trickle of saliva from the corner of my smudged lips. They think I have no shame, no self-respect, but they are the ones I have no respect for. Their lack of willpower is pathetic. It's just too easy, like shooting fish in a barrel.

I am a big mouth and a big tease. The truth is I haven't slept around as much as everyone thinks. I find some twisted satisfaction in trashing my own reputation. It's the only way I know how to be somebody. I would be happy to be Seth's girlfriend if he would stop dangling me on such a tenuous, frayed rope. I could stay on a leash if one were offered, but this is a no man's land of secret rendezvous and push-and-pull torment. I can't help lashing out and acting in defiance.

The first time I sleep with a stranger is one of those 'I don't care' acts of defiance. He's not in my usual circle of friends. I see him watching me in the garden from the balcony. He has a bad boy reputation and I want to give him a taste of his own medicine. I take my clothes off and slip into the shadow-covered pool. There is enough moonlight to see I am naked; I like knowing that he is watching me. I go back to the party with my dress clinging to my wet body. I want the opposite of intimacy. I don't want to know his name or offer up pointless small talk. I want to play a role. I like speeding away in his little black vintage sports car. It is the idea of this scenario playing out to which I am drawn, but I am left feeling numb. I feel no desire, no emotion. I don't even know why I do it.

I put on a convincing bad girl act in public, but I leave parties alone at night, driving my grandmother's battered Mazda, drunkenly singing heartbreak songs. I sob hot tears into my pillow and wait for the nights Seth, drunk out of his mind, will slurrily call, "Frensheee" from below my second-floor flat. Trampling on the flower beds, he will climb up the balcony, through my window and grope for me in the dark. He cries too sometimes and says he loves me, but why can't he say it when he is sober? How can he go out with the girl the boys talk about in the locker room? He wishes we'd met at another time in our lives when we were older. I wish my heart did not feel so bruised and tender and I could go back and undo this mess.

CHAPTER 9

SUMMER FLING

Then there is Joshua. A sweet escape from the angst and torment. I've finished my second year at university and he fills my summer holiday with great adventure. Seth has gone camping and fishing in Botswana with my dad, who now calls himself Kalahari Keith. Dad has never really settled in South Africa and can't return to a 'vandalised Black-run' Zimbabwe, so he has found another country to idolise.

I have joined a dance troupe with a motley crew of dancers, including a token Black person to play the sangoma in the African numbers. An extremely wealthy American has come to build a theme park about 60 kilometres outside Pietermaritzburg. He believes in the American dream, creating opportunities in South Africa and saving the wildlife. He is expecting hundreds of visitors to flock to his American bush dream. The other name for Pietermaritzburg is Sleepy Hollow. It's an agricultural community and a university town that empties in holidays.

Folks may come out of curiosity but there are only a few hundred thousand people in the area and most can't afford to catch the bus to Safari World, let alone the entrance fee. There's no shortage of money to throw at building an American version of an African village, wild rides and three Zippitty-Doodah shows by a local dance crew complete with the sangoma. We are paid R3,500 for three months of song and dance work.

Joshua is one of the dancers. He is a born-again Christian and surprisingly hot for a Jesus freak. He's tall and lean but not skinny. He has a smooth complexion, the colour of dark honey and a beaming white smile. He's also a masterful flirt, subtle enough to disguise this cool Christian do-gooder vibe he has going. I don't buy it. He looks so sexy in his white vest, strumming 'Kumbaya' on his guitar. So wholesome. This is going to be fun.

We just click. We joke and rag each other mercilessly. He sings Jesus songs and I tell him to let go and Carpe Diem. Life's too short to be a prude. It's refreshing to stop obsessing about Seth and have some fun. I wish I could fall in love with Joshua, and I try my best to. He's trying so hard to be pure and chaste. It's quite charming, but he doesn't stand a chance against my relentless flirting. There's enough sexual tension in the air to light up a small town.

We swim in the dam, go for sundown picnics and heavy petting in lonely grasslands. We go roaring around his farm on terrifying motorcycle rides. We spend hours talking, crying and laughing, touching, fumbling, kissing and almost making love. When he finally gives in and I have broken his resolve, the moment is bittersweet and painful. The look of disappointment on his face stings like a slap on the face. Our friendship is never the same. I have taken something he didn't want to give.

One day, we are sitting on the grass outside a Caltex garage, drinking icy Cokes from the bottle. I stare at my big toe poking out of my dancing shoes and scratch a stick in the ground. I am due to go back to university in a few weeks. I fear this fling is the final nail in the coffin of my tumultuous relationship with Seth and I also have no idea what I am doing with my life. Josh is going to London with his guitar and a backpack. He says, "Why don't you come?" I laugh and we start making plans as if we are just throwing fantasies in the air and letting them fall to the ground. Something sticks, a seed is planted. I roll the idea around in my head. The more I think about it, the more I realise this is no joke. I have just earned enough money for a plane ticket. I am dropping out. I am going to London.

My parents don't take the news very well. I vaguely hear them ranting about student loans and throwing my life away. It's just background noise, nothing will make me change my mind. My dad signed for the student loan and says I must never ask for money again. If I want to study in the future, I'll have to pay for it myself. I am financially disowned. I use my student loan to buy a backpack, sleeping bag and hiking boots. I am fully prepared to survive the streets of London.

I know two things for certain. If I leave, I will either get over Seth once and for all, or he will beg me to come home and confess his undying love for me. I'm hoping for the latter. Then we will marry, have two adorable children and live in a country house with a barn that I will convert into an art studio. Regardless of our future, I am being pulled to London as if my entire life depends on it. I must go.

I'll be going alone as Joshua already left a few weeks ago. I have his cousin's number scribbled in my notebook and the number of a digs in a suburb called Wimbledon, inhabited by South African travellers. I've been told I can crash there for a few nights when I arrive. I have £150 in travellers' cheques. I'll fly to Amsterdam first. The crossover from Amsterdam to England by bus and ferry will cost me £80. I will have £70 left and less than a week to find work and accommodation. I am 19 years old.

Although I am secretly terrified, it's too late to back out now. I say tearful goodbyes to my parents, younger sisters and Seth. I promise to write. I sit alone in the Greyhound bus; it departs at midnight for Johannesburg. I stare out the small window at the black hills rolling past and the skeletons of lonely trees. Tears stream down my face. Eventually I fall asleep, waking at dawn as we arrive at Jan Smuts Airport.

CHAPTER 10

LONDON

January '89

Victoria Station in London is an onslaught to my senses. I stand dumbstruck as streams of nameless humans in trench coats swirl around me, moving at a frenetic pace. Where are they going in such a hurry? I'm stuck for an eternity on the same spot as people jostle past me. Everything I own is on my back. I search for clues as to what to do, wondering how to navigate my way through the crowds to the ticket machine, which looks like a ticking bomb I need to diffuse. I don't know how to buy a subway ticket. Three days ago, I made a phone call from South Africa to a total stranger in London, asking if I could sleep on his couch. I have no idea where Wimbledon is.

A station official must have noticed me looking like a deer in the headlights. He offers to assist me. He's kind and grandfatherly, a distinguished Black man with a smart uniform punctuated with shiny brass buttons. When he speaks, I am taken aback by his beautiful British accent. I am overwhelmed with gratitude for his help and clutch my ticket, paying careful attention to the lady telling me to "Mind the gap" as I step onto my first ride on the London underground.

I am terrified to remove my backpack and so I sit strangely upright, perched on the edge of the seat, swaying rhythmically to the movement of the train. I nervously check every station we pass. I try to seek out a friendly face among the commuters to make eye contact, but everyone is reading a newspaper or quickly averts their gaze to avoid my inane grin. I will soon learn only psychopaths smile at strangers on the tube.

When Wimbledon is announced, I exit the station and trudge up a long hill, eventually reaching the address I have. I almost sob with relief when someone opens the door and says, "Howzit!"

The digs is a two-storey hovel. It reeks of stale beer and cigarettes. I count fifteen people crashing there and have no idea where they sleep. I am offered three nights on the floor if I can find a spot not strewn with suitcases, beer bottles or bodies. We all head off to Leicester Square to drink expensive beer and talk rubbish to Australians. I have two days to find a job.

The following day, I manage to find work through an agency as an au pair in a little country village. The family live in a mansion the size of an average Sandton home in Johannesburg. It has sculpted hedges instead of concrete walls and electric fencing. It smells of gardenias and old money. The kids are brats. They are in clear need of a good smack. There's nothing like a good wallop across the back of your bare bottom to recalibrate a kid. The wife is dripping with pearls and forced sincerity, insisting I make myself at home. I am regaled with stories of the previous South African au pair, whom they simply adored. She was "part of the family".

It's a miserable two weeks. My ironing is "despicable". I silently scream, "I am not your effing maid!" But that is exactly what I am. The hired help. A servant dressed up as a "family companion".

The children and I don't like each other. I don't feel at home. I try to make the kids play outside barefoot. The two-year-old screams blue murder as if I'd set him down on hot coals. His soft pink feet have never walked on grass before. Jeez, what is wrong with these people? Within a fortnight, I am fired. I am told I am not a "good fit" for the family.

I really need to find Joshua.

CHAPTER 11
RATTLE AND HUM
February '89

I've been staying in London with Joshua and his cousin in a shoebox bedsit. We share one room and one lumpy sleeper couch. There is a cramped communal bathroom. It must have originally been a broom cupboard before the house was broken up into cheap accommodation. You can shower and pee in the toilet at the same time. The three of us can fit in the kitchen if one of us climbs onto the window ledge. It is messy and smells, cramped and awkward, but we tell ourselves that we are living the dream.

My au pair money is dwindling. I need to find a job. It will not be acting as the nanny again. My White ego is too fragile for the English class system. I remember a conversation with one of the posh mommies at Clifton School in Durban years ago. I must have made a mental note and filed the information away somewhere. Mrs Baxter Smith was from what's known as an ODF, an Old Durban Family with proper old money and connections. She was also a raging alcoholic. She once mentioned something about being a hostess.

"Daaarrrling," she drawled, "in the fabulous sixties, a nice-looking girl could work as a hostess in London. There were upmarket exclusive gentleman's clubs. Just look pretty and serve cocktails. You can earn a fortune in tips." This sounded like a job made just for me. No more snotty, spoilt brats, plus I know how to smile and look pretty.

※

I'm sitting on the train, contemplating my survival options. My Walkman is blasting U2's latest CD, *Rattle and Hum*, "...but I still haven't found what I'm looking for...". I know when I am being checked out and I lift my eyes to look directly into soulful eyes and skin the shade of dark roasted coffee. I blush and look away from a young man full of swag and self-confidence. But I can't help stealing glances at him. I totally ignore unspoken British social protocol and street smarts by making eye contact and giving him a coy smile.

He ambles over, exuding coolness, and sits so close I can smell his High Street cologne. He stretches out his elegant hand to greet me. I am now up close to a new and unfamiliar stranger that I have been noticing in this multi-cultural city. It's not just the punks, goths, transsexuals, skinheads, heroin addicts or any of the other subcultures turning my head in the streets. This is something entirely different. An urban jungle person that I have not yet encountered in my life, someone who had no place in my former world, someone who does not and cannot exist where I come from.

This is a well-dressed, educated, articulate, self-assured Black male.

When he says, "Hi gorgeous," in his British accent and flashes a bright smile, I am taken aback. He thinks I'm unsettled because he has approached me, and he has misread my signals. I am unsettled because my narrow, White, privileged, racist ideas are being assaulted with a blunt object. From where I come, Black men look down at their feet when they speak to me. They call me 'Madam', they speak with thick accents in broken English. They are not educated, they are not self-assured. They are beaten, broken, angry and violent. They mow our lawns and put petrol in our cars. If they get too clever or try to take charge they are thrown in prison and sent to Robben Island.

I am intrigued by this stranger and accept his invitation to go for a drink.

I hang out with Richard a few times. He is funny, charming, intelligent, attractive and impressed at my ability to chug down a pint of beer. I must be an interesting specimen to him too. A bona-fide White girl fresh out of apartheid South Africa. He asks a lot of questions. My answers are ignorant and defensive. I am so tired of everyone thinking I am racist because of where I come from. I say things like, "It's not about race, we are too different, we don't get along, it's cultural. We'd live separately even if there were no laws keeping us apart."

What I mean is, "We are better, superior and more advanced. Black people are inferior and backward." I never say these things out loud, they are thinly hidden, insidious, putrid entrails wrapped in rose-tinted paper and tied up with a white ribbon.

I haven't learnt to think for myself yet and so I still spew out the garbage I have been spoon-fed since I was born. I have never had a Black friend. I may as well have tried to befriend an alien, our worlds are so far apart. All my carefully constructed ideas about society, race and politics are a house built of ugly straw and my inexperience of integrated society in a new and cosmopolitan city is going to burn the flimsy house down. I have come from a place so backward and deformed that we may as well have just crawled out of the swamps. But the mind shift is so great, the mental jump is so impossibly vast for me to make, that I simply divide Black people into two categories. English: educated, cultured and civilised. African: ignorant, backward, no culture.

One Sunday morning, sitting in Richard's apartment and reading the back pages of *The Sun*, he leans forward to kiss me. I recoil and in that split second, I cannot disguise my violent reaction. It has come from deep inside my gut like the yellow bile gagged and heaved after emptying your stomach of its contents. It has come from the place of terror, lying awake waiting for the savages to tear us apart. I am strangled with the fear of being violated by Black lips. The idea of kissing a Black man is so taboo even thinking about it is a betrayal of everything I know.

The rest of the morning is littered with overly polite and uncomfortable exchanges. No amount of tea will mend the moment that I bared my teeth and snarled at him like a chained dog. It is the last time that I see him.

CHAPTER 12

HOSTESS
March '89

"Hostess Wanted."

It's written in black and white, so small when I skim through the classified employment section of the newspaper that I almost miss it. Two words. I read them a few times to make sure I am not imagining it. "Hostess Wanted." I call the number from a phone booth and speak to Alice. I have an interview on Sunday afternoon.

I exit the train station nearest to the address I have been given. The street is empty. It's Sunday in a business district. In the week it will be bustling with men in pin-striped suits, carrying hand-stitched leather briefcases, hurrying to important meetings and lunches in trendy cafés. Tall, formal buildings loom over me, squeezing out the grey sky and casting deep shadows.

The sound of my footsteps echoes. I turn into a quiet side avenue and check street numbers till I arrive at a single black door with a brass knocker. There is no sign above, no windows to peer into. Just a black door. I press the buzzer on the intercom, wondering if I am at the correct address. There is a crackle and I respond to the same voice I heard on the telephone. "Hello Alice, it's Terry."

I feel like Alice in Wonderland, behind the dark door which is like the official entrance to a rabbit hole, burrowed beneath the stiff buildings staring down at me. The door clicks open and down I go. A staircase takes me into a small bar lounge.

Alice is sitting at the bar. She is dressed in black. She has porcelain skin, white hair and icy blue eyes. She does not try to put me at ease or make me feel welcome. She explains what is expected and seems indifferent to my response. I will either take the job on her terms or leave, it does not seem to matter what I decide. While she is explaining how the club operates, my eyes scan the room. A small mahogany bar, emerald-green velvet banquettes, dark panelled walls, a small office to the side of the narrow room, brass lamps, the smell of stale liquor and cigarette smoke, faded carpets and mirrors from above the wood panels to the ceiling.

I vaguely hear her say "... private men's club ... exclusive ... You are to entertain the customers... They buy champagne you need to drink ... earn a tip of £50 ... regulars ... private booths..." and finally, "You need to wear lingerie. Be here Monday at 6pm if you want the job."

It seems too easy. Too good to be true. £50 to drink champagne and wear lingerie? How hard can it be? While studying, I was in a local theatre production in Pietermaritzburg. I did a mock strip tease dance to "You can leave your hat on", by Joe Cocker. I did a duet with my friend Belinda. The slapstick variety style show took place in the local town hall in front of an audience of family and friends. I had worn a silk camisole with matching knickers under a trench coat and a black top hat. It doesn't alarm me in the slightest to wear lingerie in front of people.

I don't want to think about what else is expected at the "gentleman's club" so I shut off that part of my brain and greedily grab onto the things I want to believe.

I want to believe this will be an easy way to make cash and it will be a little naughty but mostly harmless. I want to believe it will be like playing a part in a play in a local am-dram show. I want to believe in adventure. I want to believe I am savvy enough to keep my wits about me and that I will leave if things get out of hand.

On Monday evening at 6pm sharp I am sitting on the emerald banquette. I am wearing the cream silky French knickers and matching camisole I had the good sense to pack. My skin still has a hint of days under the baking African sun. I am satisfied my ensemble is quite tasteful, even classy, which seems appropriate as this is a "gentleman's" establishment.

I am a bit self-conscious and apprehensive. Just new girl jitters. Like school, I tell myself. I pretend I have waited in rooms like this before. I am hoping I can pull off a look of sultry nonchalance and try not to bite my fingernails.

The room appears more exotic than on the day of my interview. Grubby stains hidden in velvet shadows, stale smells choked out with cheap perfume and wary anticipation. The lights bounce off the mirrored walls like a carnival house. The long narrow lounge is mirrored on each side and reflects the opposite wall, creating the illusion that it is bigger and grander in scale. I can see multiple images of myself staring back across the room, like split personalities that I can watch disappear and reappear. I glance at one of my reflections when I think the other one is not looking, the way I watch strangers on the train. Careful not to make eye contact. Careful not to get caught. I watch myself with curious but guarded eyes. I am watching her, watching me watching her. I am her and she is me. Waiting to see what the girl in the mirror will do.

There are eight of us sitting like silk and satin wall flowers, lined up along the edge of the carnival house hoping to be chosen to dance. I look at the girl who has worked here the longest. She is easy to identify. She has an air of bitter indifference, scornful lips and empty eyes giving nothing away. There is another girl who looks new like me. She is also foreign, I think. Dark hair, dark eyes and dark skin. She looks lovely but when I smile at her, her eyes narrow suspiciously, and she looks away.

In the corner is a thin girl with her arms tucked in like bird wings. She looks frail, like she has fallen out of a tree and landed here. Crouched and timid. I don't think she will be here for long. She reminds me of the baby sparrows I used to rescue when they fell from their muddy nests in the roof rafters. I put them in empty tissue boxes and fed them Pronutro from a medicine dropper. They never survived. Once, I put my little rescued bird in the oven warming drawer as a makeshift incubator. You could still see its heart beating through thin, puckered featherless skin. Later, when my mother went to put dinner in the drawer, she found my teeny, tiny baby bird curled up in its tissue box. It was warm and safe as it slowly baked to death.

We sit still and aloof in our strangely lit waiting room. In a green warming drawer. Little baby sparrows. Sitting ducks.

※

There is one barman behind the counter. The door of the office is closed. I have not met the owner yet. The barman puts on a CD. It's British soul band Hot Chocolate.

"I believe in miracles,
Where you from
You sexy thing, sexy thing."

Hot Chocolate plays night after night and soon I will know every single word to every single song. It will be the soundtrack accompanying me as I slip off the edge, surrendering the last shreds of my tattered innocence. Swimming out into deep cold water, far beyond safety to the familiar current of risk and rebellion.

"I believe in miracles,

Where you from ... you sexy thing."

The doorbell rings and it sounds the call to the opening of the theatre of the bizarre. Everyone comes alive like wind-up dolls and the room starts to spin with false laughter and seduction.

The first member to arrive at the gentleman's club starts with a drink at the bar. He is squat, bald, pasty and sits perched on the barstool. It is his chance to look around and examine his options. I feel his eyes roaming over our bodies. We sit casually, knowing we are being evaluated. "Pick Me! Don't pick me!"

A lingerie line-up.

I am caught between an eagerness to impress and an instinct that silently screams "RUN!" My gut tells me more than charm and champagne will be exchanged. I don't move. I don't even flinch. I sit frozen and still, strangely calm. Watching. I am reluctant to leave. I am unable to turn my eyes away. I am drawn in like a moth to a flame, unaware something is stalking in the flickering shadows.

I want to know what happens behind the closed curtains at the end of the room. What happens in the private booths? Curiosity burns, engulfing any sense of foreboding. Seduced by intrigue, I want to see what will happen. Just one night. Just one peep. Should I leave? Should I flee? Should I get the hell out of here? I tell myself I will just wait and see. I tell myself that I can be an observer. I can sit on the sidelines and watch. I can be an undercover investigator. A visitor. A bystander. A voyeur.

Liar. Liar. Liar.

Curiosity killed the kitty.

The gentleman disappears into a booth with the older girl. She seems scornfully amused. I don't think I am hiding my nerves well.

Is she gloating? The cat who ate the canary. She's popular with the customers and when she has left, someone explains why.

"She'll do anything with them."

"It's not allowed but it's up to you, as long as you don't get caught," says someone else.

The establishment makes money selling cheap champagne for the exorbitant price of £250. It's a scam everyone is privy to. The customers know they are not just buying champagne. We are paid to swallow as much of it down as we can without puking.

"She's got her regulars," says another. I want to know more but I am unsure how to ask the right questions. I do not want to look stupid.

I am soon invited to a private booth by a customer, which makes me feel a heady cocktail of relief and terror. I am grateful he wants the company of two girls, so I am not alone with him. The private booth is small, forcing intimacy. It is candlelit. The banquette is curved, a half-moon around a small cocktail table, with plants on each side. The wall behind it is mirrored.

We sit on either side of the customer, facing the closed curtains. After a few awkward moments and gulps of champagne, I relax a little and something in me switches gear, something instinctive. Click. Click. My natural ambition kicks in.

I am eager to please and do my job to the best of my ability. My private school education has groomed me well. Reach for the stars! Always give your best! Be the best!

Failure is not an option. I can do this. I will be exceptional. I will impress and charm and delight. I will drink as much champagne as I can.

We consume three bottles between the two of us. The boss is impressed. I have earned my £50 fee plus the same in a tip. £100, which equals R1,989 in 2021. It's more than I earned dancing three shows every day for three months. It is more than the cost of my return plane ticket.

Hasn't it been harmless? Hasn't it been easy? I can do this. I can do it excellently! A bit of pawing and groping, flattery and sexy banter. Tonight, no actual lewd acts or sexual services are performed. It's a fine line, a tightrope, and I am sure I can teeter on the edge. I can dance around the licking flames and not get burnt. Why not fleece money off rich, lecherous fools? It's as easy as shooting fish in a barrel.

The moment I could have left has passed. It slipped through my fingers the moment I pulled open the curtain to the booth and sat down to entertain a stranger. It will never come back. It can never be undone. I swallowed the pill. I turned the key. I crossed the line. I went down the rabbit hole. I gulped down champagne and the lies I will start telling myself to make this all okay.

'Creeping Normality', also known as 'Landscape Amnesia', is the term used to describe the way monumental changes can be accepted as normal if the changes occur in minuscule, barely perceptible increments. It is best illustrated by the popular Boiling Frog experiment. A useful metaphor. The premise is, if a frog is placed in tepid water and the water is gradually heated to boiling point, the frog will not jump out but will instead boil to death.

In 1882, William Thompson Sedgwick successfully confirmed that the hypothesis could be proved under specific conditions. The frog must be heated over a much longer time and at extremely gradual changes in a temperature of less than 0.002 degrees Celsius. In two and a half hours the frog was found dead, not having even so much as moved or struggled.

I cannot say when I first exchanged a sexual favour for money. It seems odd that I am not able to pinpoint the exact moment. I should be able to remember the person, the shape of his face, an identifying feature, the words forming the negotiation. It should be etched on my mind in blinding technicolour.

It seems implausible that something so far-reaching would just happen casually, and yet, there were just moments that slipped by in incremental compromises. I can't recall the first one. It's lost and buried. It has disintegrated into a million fractions of time: an inappropriate touch, a hand not pushed away, fingers slipping under my camisole, dirty suggestions whispered in my ear, a hundred-pound note slipped into my panties, a trouser zip undone.

At first, I watch and listen. I can hear the sounds in the booths next door. I can hear when conversation distils to just the sounds of breath and the friction of clothing. I hear the strangulated groans of pleasure.

It is not long before I am in the same room with another girl who is touching and stroking a customer. Soon I am the one touching the exposed pink erection thrusting out of the teeth of a zip, demanding attention. I understand what is expected and I do it. It is mostly just a quick, furtive hand job or if he is lucky, a blowjob. Tedious touching and groping. A little kissing, which I begin to avoid. I don't like kissing older men. It's gross.

The other stuff is inane, I can shut myself off, blot it out and do it while letting my mind wander off…sushi or curry later, hope he finishes quickly, pathetic pervert. There is no existential or moral debate.

At first, there is no guilt or shame. There are no sleepless nights twisting in anguish. Just moment after moment of compromises sucking me down the rabbit hole. I am carried along a current. I do not struggle against it. I just let it carry me along. Champagne-dazed and intoxicated, floating numbly in a green velvet room that dresses up sleaze in a shadow of glamour. I don't jump out of the water. Landscape Amnesia. Boiling Frog Syndrome.

CHAPTER 13

PARTNERS IN CRIME
March '89

I have been working at the club for just a few nights when I meet Sally. She has a wholesome girl-next-door look. She's slim with sandy blonde hair and green-blue eyes which change colour like the moods of the sea. Her milky skin is sprinkled with freckles. She embodies both ancient witch and innocent waif, with a dash of rock chic. It's a dangerous package. I find her irresistible. She has this gritty confidence, a way of moving through life as if she is the one making up all the rules. She navigates this world with ease, nothing rattles her. In daylight, there are fine, almost imperceptible lines under her eyes and lips that suggest she has experienced the rougher edges of life. She is twenty-seven. I instinctively know we will be partners in crime. We recognise something wild and greedy in each other and become inseparable. Our chemistry will be the kind that turns heads, blows things up, and brings about catastrophe.

Joshua and his cousin are becoming increasingly suspicious of what exactly I do at work, and it is getting harder to convincingly lie about what my job as a hostess involves. I fumble back in the early hours of each morning to sleep off several bottles of champagne and the incessant pawing of lascivious creeps. I curl into a pile of clothes and blankets in the corner. I can't stay here. I feel guilty about my double life. They are suspicious and concerned. I am vague and brush off their questions or change the subject. I cannot tell them the truth. They are born-again Christians. The Jesus songs and kumbaya guitar strumming is grinding on my nerves.

There is nothing romantic going on with Joshua. When I first moved in with him, we had spent a few days hiking through the countryside in perpetual drizzle, broke and miserable, sleeping in fields and barns.

In April, he takes me to see Hugh Masekela perform in a jazz club for my twentieth birthday. I weep White girl tears, homesick for Africa. I never see Josh again.

I find an affordable bedsit in Kilburn, a cheap, unsavoury neighbourhood. It's bizarre to me that in London I can walk down one avenue, lined with oak trees and gracious apartments, turn the corner, cross the bridge and find myself on a derelict street that looks like it survived the apocalypse.

I don't understand a place that is not clearly segregated. Why is privilege so close to poverty? The street where I now live is littered with broken glass, cars with missing limbs and people who never smile. The room is dull, cold and feels like a bunker. Built only for survival. The kitchen and bathroom are supposedly shared but I never see another soul. The only human interaction I have is with the construction workers on the building site next door, mostly whistles and cat calling. The foreman comes for tea sometimes and we sit at the faded Formica table.

I spend as little time as I can there and look forward to nightfall so I can drown in champagne and be with the dysfunctional family I have become a part of. I can dress up and play adult games.

I spend most days exploring the city. I get lost in the art galleries, the museums and the markets, the department stores and the bookstores. I like being alone, drifting and wandering around a city with no edges. I imagine my life as sophisticated and glamorous. Anonymity has become a salve. All boundaries are dissolving. I once wanted to be seen, now I feel liberated by invisibility. No one knows, no one cares.

I am being swallowed, disappearing into a city willing to eat me alive. I am feasting on money, mayhem and manipulation, my heart is hardening and my bohemian, carpe diem, fuck society, fierce, no rules apply, do what I want, don't give shit, non-conformist alter ego is driving the car.

I often stay over with Sally. It's getting harder to go back to my grim little bedsit. She lives in a studio flat below ground level on Baker Street. We watch legs walk past the window you need to stand on the bed to see out of. It's small but cosy and we sit in our pyjamas drinking tea till late in the afternoon. Sally is in love with an Australian rock star who she's had an affair with but who is now on tour, so she can't be with him.

I am still in love with Seth, hoping he's missing me too. We share our heartache for the lovers we have each left miles away. Then we brush aside our sweetheart recollections and get dressed for work, moving seamlessly from nostalgia to a parallel universe. I keep my heart and dreams separate from this life, careful not to get my precious memories and girlish fantasies tarnished. I wrap them gently in tissue paper to preserve them for stolen moments of longing.

I am naive, not understanding what is inevitable. My lie will slowly poison my fragile dreams till they are just a fleeting scent, letters read till the folds are worn and grubby.

I primarily came to London to get over him, but I can't help myself longing for him. I keep hoping my absence will make him want me back. I am not ready to give up on a happily-ever-after with him.

    Seth and I write to one another. I know the words of his letters by heart, read over and over, murmured with eyes blurry from salty tears. Notes and photographs carried from place to place like passports to a lost country. I don't understand how impossible it will be to keep my dreams safe in tissue paper. If I can stash everything neatly in boxes, making sure the contents never jumble together, maybe I can function. In my immaturity I think I can keep my call-girl activities a secret and pick up where I left off with Seth when I get home. I am simultaneously stupidly inexperienced and brash. It seems an improbable combination and one that will prove lethal. The most dangerous lies are the ones I tell myself.

CHAPTER 14

THE TOAD

March '89

The clients who come to the club want discretion. They are willing to pay for it. They like the business district, quiet and desolate at night. The private black door. There are no flashing neon signs promising tits and titillation. It's small and intimate. You are known by your first name. The barman knows your drink. Home away from home.

The members are businessmen, bankers, entrepreneurs, lawyers, judges, and members of Parliament. The well-heeled, well-to-do and well-connected. Strictly by appointment only. Customers cannot be seen taking us home. We are to keep them here buying champagne. Selling alcohol is legal. Prostitution is not. I am learning a few tricks. I don't need to drink all the champagne, just a bottle. The rest is tipped into the pot plants when no one is looking. The ice bucket too. Private arrangements are discreetly made, phone numbers exchanged. Secret rendezvous planned outside of club hours.

There are regulars who come to the club. They are the cash cows and sugar daddies. Highly prized and sought after. If you find one who wants to rescue you, take you home to rehabilitate you like a bird with a broken wing, then you have hit the jackpot. A man is always hungry to be heroic. Alice used to be a working girl till the boss took a fancy to her. Now she interviews the girls who he will beckon into his office when she isn't around. Her icy demeanour is justified. She's been rescued and placed in a gilded cage. And she's always under threat of being replaced.

Sally and I have arranged to meet 'The Judge' on Saturday afternoon at his apartment. It's my first meeting with a private client outside the club. We arrive at his apartment block at teatime. The building is intimidating, modern and sleek. We take the elevator to avoid the suspicious eyes of the doorman.

The Judge opens the door and lets us into an apartment jarringly at odds with the modern building. It's gloomy and stale. Outdated luxury sucks the life out of the interior. Thick musty curtains hang stiffly, disapproving faces look down on us from dark photo frames. Our client is a prominent judge or politician. We aren't really paying attention. We follow him to his bedroom and the large antique bed creaks as he sinks onto the end of it. He sits slumped like an enormous albino toad.

His stringy hair is slicked to one side in a futile attempt to cover his blotchy bald head. His skin, acne scarred and patchy, is a landscape from which a bulbous nose protrudes, and skin bulges out of the neck of his olive green shirt. He is awkward and charmless. Harmless. It feels like his mum could walk in any moment with a tray of tea and crumpets while we are playing a game of 'I'll show you mine if you show me yours.' He points to photographs above his dresser of him meeting the Queen and another with him and Margaret Thatcher. We pretend to be marvellously impressed.

He unzips his pants and lets his trousers and boxers fall to the floor, exposing pale, papery skin and shrivelled knees. The rest of what is exposed emits an unwashed, sickeningly sour odour of sweat and urine which makes us gag. It is impossibly foul. We glance at each other and exchange a knowing look; this is going to require skilful manoeuvring. Our objective is clear: maximum customer satisfaction with minimal physical contact. It will not be easy, but there is no way either of us can stomach intimacy with *that* smell! Strictly hands only.

I am secretly wishing he had a surgical glove and mask fetish so I can cover my hands and nose.

We drag out the time, stripping to a sliver of underwear. Purring with flattery and flirting, we hope he does not notice we are avoiding physical contact. We touch each other instead and he drools over us, lapping up our giggling, flattering attention like a slobbering bulldog. He is oblivious, unaware we are laughing scornfully at him. The clock next to his bed ticks, marking the passing of each revolting second.

Our strategy has worked. We have used every trick to tease him into a state of glassy-eyed arousal. When I cup his repugnant testicles in my hand, I hear three ticks of the clock before he releases his satisfaction onto the carpet. I look up and see the Queen, smiling, and Margaret Thatcher looking down, formidably impressed.

We spill onto the streets shrieking with laughter. In our eyes he is the one who has degraded himself and behaved like a drooling desperate fool. We are vicious with disdain and consumed with avarice, clutching several hundred-pound notes. Tenderness suffocates in transactions reduced to mutual and greedy exploitation of lust and loneliness. We are users, manipulators, greedy grabbers, scratch your eyes out, spit on you creatures.

CHAPTER 15

THINGS I LEARN
April '89

At night, I enter through the black door as if passing through a porthole to an alternative reality. I learn to move in this world below the pavements. I catch on fast. I learn to survive. I want to know how the game is played. I instinctively understand the unwritten rules. It makes perfect sense to me that affluent businessmen need light-hearted relief and the company of a young girl who comes without any expectations. No strings whatsoever. It makes sense to me that these men want to eliminate the usual rules of engagement, the farce of pretending to want anything other than the flattering attentions of a pretty young thing, with the highest probability of a sexual encounter. A night club with the odds stacked highly in the client's favour.

I learn the art of seduction. I learn the lure of the gentleman's club is the make-believe world it conjures for the customer. Veiled in lace, barely disguised, is the delusion that he is desirable, if only for his money and power. There is a game to be played here, a farce, a theatrical production in which to stage his fantasy. An image he has torn from a dirty magazine, folded permanently inside his head. It is a place of escape where he does not have to hide or mask his lust. His desire can be laid bare without fear of judgement, ridicule or rejection.

I learn to read the customers, bending, twisting and contorting to the shape of their ideation. I can act. I have many personas on tap: coy, shy, boisterous, mysterious, silly, intelligent, assertive, compliant. I learn most men hunger for a cocktail of innocence and naughtiness. This club is tame, a 'dip your toe in' playschool to meet young girls who are not too hardcore for the clients. Grade One for Hookers.

My most valuable commodity is my youth, and I am burning it up as if it is limitless. Most of the men are in their late forties to early fifties. To a twenty-year-old girl, they are all old men. My most alluring outfit is a navy and white polka dot bustier with boxer shorts, edged with virginal white lace. Sexy, a little posh, not overtly trashy. I learn to leave something to the imagination, something to be revealed. Anticipation and discovery are powerful aphrodisiacs. Customers want to feel they have seduced you; they want a conquest, so it's best not to be too easy, too quick to give in to demands. I feign naivety, a little shock at their suggestions, fooling them into the belief I am eventually unable to resist their charm. It's a tease. They are paying for a chase. Otherwise, they would have picked up a streetwalker, flaunting herself openly on a seedy pavement corner. There is no illusion in hustling and whoring in public places. What you see is what you get. No mystery, no seduction, no art. This is different.

I learn who to avoid – the men with dead, empty cold eyes who stare right through me to the source of their hatred. Violence seething under their skins, rage just a flicker away.

I learn to drift out of my body, floating away to a safe distance, where my soul and body can function independently. Soul, spirit, body, brain, emotion severed and spliced into a zombie, half dead, half alive. Feeding and being fed upon.

I can observe myself and others. It's like watching strangers from an empty bus stop, noticing details without judgement or feeling. The veins pulsate beneath skin pulled taut, a bead of sweat, a sneer, a sigh. Leaving my body, I travel as a visitor. A voyeuristic tourist. Just passing through. Taking in the scenery, the fairground attractions, the Hall of Horrors, the spinning Ferris Wheel. It is as surreal as the wax figures in Madame Tussauds.

I am not a citizen. I can glide past unscathed as long as I loosen myself from my body and float up to the ceiling the way the dead-brought-back-to-life watch their corpses on the operating table. The parts of me I cannot be dislocated or detached from are shut away behind impenetrable barriers. Fear, loneliness, shame, regret, disgust, terror, anxiety closed behind heavy doors, slammed shut.

※

When The Gecko walks into the club one night, I am astute enough to recognise that he is a rescuer. Tall, thin, skin as pale as an albino lounge lizard. He is dressed head-to-toe in a silky shoulder-padded Armani suit, wearing a cowboy hat and bolo tie. He is as smooth and slippery as he looks. His blue eyes are sharp and bright, his goatee groomed and his Texas accent like warm syrup. He has the American confidence and swagger the British find so offensive. Slick, creepy Southern charm.

Sally and I pounce on him immediately. He has huge Sugar Daddy potential. He is a regular and we become his favourite pair. He says he is an international art dealer and a lover of beautiful objects. He comes to the club most weeks and we sit either side of his lanky body, tucked into the crooks of his arms with our legs and arms draped over him, forming one intertwined pile of limbs and luxury. We are at ease with him. He is benevolent, generous and fun to be with. We are his "Gals". He dates and courts us, needing to form a bond of sorts to mask the harsh reality that our dirty intimacy is bought. We can play this game. He is the patron, the kind uncle, the worldly-wise guide. We intend to exploit his desire to take care of us to the maximum.

On one of his visits to the club, we are all draped over one another when he pulls out a small snuff vial and a teeny silver spoon. He deftly tips a little pile of white powder onto the cocktail table. Cocaine. He wants us to try some. Just a little sniff. He uses his credit card to smooth the white powder to a fine dust and carves the pile into three neat rows. I am nervous and hesitant but also curious. I always said "No" to drugs. He assures us it is harmless.

It is the first time in my twenty years on earth that I've been in contact with hard drugs. Till this moment I've only seen weed the Joburg kids smoked at the abandoned quarry near varsity. I have long forgotten how to say "No" and it seems pointless to worry about consequences anymore. He offers a little pinch of dust.

"Rub it on your gums," he suggests. Teething gel to numb the pain. I dab a little on my finger to tentatively sniff. I try a little bit more. Sniff a little harder. Nothing. I wait for a rush of sensation, a euphoria of sorts. I don't like the idea of complete loss of control or a trip to oblivion. The thought scares me and keeps me from crossing the line between drunk and dead drunk, teetering precariously on the verge of being wasted. I am already so wanton, so reckless and free-spirited without the help of alcohol. I loathe hangovers and am prone to migraines. I like to have at least some of my wits about me.

This white powder does not feel like it's having any effect. I take the bill rolled into a tube like a miniature newspaper and snort the whole line, half up each nostril. I feel a burning sensation like I've sniffed pepper. Then it drips to the back of my throat. I try not to swallow. Snorting without swallowing will take more practice. A pleasant numbing feeling, but still no fireworks. I am feeling a bit let down ... but then it rises gradually, not a rush but a burn. A deep red heat and energy radiates from me. I am filled with a feeling of immense power. I am invincible. Unstoppable. Fucking brilliant and gorgeous. My mind and tongue and wit are sharp as flashing silver. Hyper focus. Hyperactive. The room is golden, the velvet sumptuous, the flicker of the candle mesmerising.

I look at everything as if seeing it for the first time. This paltry booth cannot contain me. I want to explode, to dance, to scratch, to thrash, to fuck, to throw my head back and scream. This letting go is intoxicating, nothing remains but some essence of me, some primordial femme to sway and pulsate in this one singular moment in time. Any residue of decorum or inhibition, already no more than a flimsy gauze, a whisper on my skin, is ripped off and flung into the fire. I have given myself over completely like a wild banshee covered in smears of war paint and streaks of mud, stomping and heaving in the light of fire and dust. Fairy dust. Ash.

White powder magic to smooth the rough edges, shine up the deadening dullness, to make tolerable the humiliation of being just the body, the hand, the thigh, the mouth, to be rubbed, groped, spilled on and emptied into. The white powder fairy Godmother, changing rats and lizards into footmen, pumpkins into carriages. White powder mayhem. White powder energy, direct line to the buzz, the on switch, the go-go-go, the party all night, the we-are-so-beautiful, the who-gives-a-shit, the-take-it-too-far bridge to snow-dusted Narnia.

CHAPTER 16

QUARANTINED
April '89

Mornings are usually groggy and sluggish with hangovers but today I can hardly lift my head from the pillow. It's pounding louder than the jackhammers on the building site next to my bunker bedsit. It's probably just the flu.

Two days pass and I am still in bed, sick and feverish like a dog. I haven't eaten or left the flat. There's no food in the fridge. I manage to hobble weakly to the bathroom and stripping off my fever-soaked clothes, I notice two blisters on my thighs. Odd. Bathe, back to bed.

I toss and turn with fever and discomfort. Something is not right. My body is on fire. I change again and to my horror I notice that my torso is covered in what looks like insect bites. Flea bites? Bedbugs? I am horrified. Terrified. I'm so ill, something must be horribly wrong with me.

I consider all the possibilities and conclude God himself has rained down a pestilence upon me. I am being eaten alive with some vile venereal disease. I need to get help. I consider my options. Lie here and rot to death, covered in filthy sores like a leper, or suffer the humiliation of going to an NHS doctor who will immediately know I am a promiscuous harlot.

I sit in the waiting room of the local NHS hospital, filled with dread but resolved to endure the impending disgrace and indignity. There is too much fluorescent white light here, too much exposure.

The doctor is a young Indian man. I avoid eye contact. I am sure the words "DIRTY SLUT" are glued to my forehead. Perched on the examination table in a starched green gown, I await judgement. Without hesitation, the doctor announces that I have chicken pox and must immediately be sent to a quarantine facility.

I am so relieved you could knock me down with a feather. I hardly hear him explaining that I will immediately be taken by ambulance to a special unit somewhere on the outskirts of London. There is a chicken pox outbreak and I need to be isolated.

"Do not go home. Do not pack. Everything you need will be provided. Do you want to notify anyone?"

Within thirty minutes I am in an ambulance driving through London to who-knows-where. Contaminated goods on board. I cannot see where I am being taken and when I get there, bodies in white suits arrive to wheel me out on the stretcher. I am rolled through a bleak, sterile building. It looks more like a prison than a hospital. The white suits push me down a long corridor, passing door after door after door until we stop in front of one of them and I am wheeled in. I am told to get off the stretcher and wait until the suits have exited. I must change into the hospital-issue pyjamas on the bed and dispose of my clothing in the plastic bag. I must not bathe for the next three days. Food and medicine will be brought to the room. The door does not open from the inside. There are no windows.

"Try not to scratch."

The room is barely big enough to fit a single iron hospital bed, a white metal side table and a chair. There is a bathroom attached. Food and medicine are pushed through the glass hatch on a stainless-steel tray by the people in white biohazard suits. Once a day a white suit takes my temperature and blood pressure and fills out a chart on a clipboard. Everything I have touched, worn, slept on or eaten with, is disposed into plastic bags like radioactive waste.

I am weak, isolated and lonely to the bones. Literally no one knows where I am. I don't even know where I am. I can make a phone call but who should I call? The phone is wheeled into my room. It's covered in plastic. I wear surgical gloves to use it. I try Sally and leave a message on her answering machine. There's no point, no one can visit anyway. Why call Mom and Dad and cause unnecessary worry?

Chicken pox pustules have ravished my body. I search my limbs for any unblemished patches of skin. My eyelids bulge with inflamed red sores. My mouth is swollen from them. My toes, underarms, genitals, even the soles of my feet, are all under the onslaught of this viral attack. I lie here in torment, my face monstrous with pink calamine lotion and seeping, weepy sores. The itchiness is unbearable, a constant affliction. I am living in the twilight zone. Zombie land.

Eventually, ten days later I am discharged and taken back to the NHS hospital. The pox marks have dried up and formed scabs. I look hideous but if I can resist scratching the scarring will not be too bad. I am broke and exhausted.

While I was in quarantine, I've had time to think about my life and I've made a few decisions. During the day, I am going to learn how to type and then do a desktop publishing course. I dream of a brilliant future. But for now, I need a plan. For now, I will have to earn quick cash and the only way I know is at the gentleman's club. Thankfully, it's dark in there. And there's always make-up to cover up the scabs and scars.

CHAPTER 17

WHITE CLOUDS AND TURTLE DOVES

May '89

Sally and I are tethered at the hip. A yin and yang. Bright and black, positive and negative. She leads, I follow. Heaven and Earth, feminine and masculine, darkness and light, passive and active, receptacle and penetrator. The tiger and the dragon, burnt orange and azure blue, streams of water and thrusting mountain peaks. The broken and unbroken line. We mould together into a two-headed Medusa. Conjoined Siamese twins at a peep show. Shape shifters. We read each other's body language, signals, eyes and moods. I yield to her; she is my older sister. I yield to her street smarts, her tough as nails self-assurance. A dangerous partnership has formed. It gives us the balls to stray from the club and think about venturing out on our own.

We are earning enough money to be able to move in together. We can pool our income and potential together and find somewhere more uptown. I can finally move out of the grim basement bedsit. We need a posh place where we can entertain Gecko and other wealthy regulars. We are off to look at an apartment advertised in the paper. A fully furnished and renovated modern Edwardian apartment within walking distance from Angel station in Islington.

The street is elegantly curved and lined with Edwardian buildings in chalky shades of grey and white against milky skies. Occasional piles of rubble and a few building skips are evidence of the street's ongoing gentrification.

We meet the owner of the flat and the builder responsible for all the renovations in the area. His wild grey hair and dusty appearance explains his building occupation but does not explain his obsession with all things Edwardian. He can't resist showing off his projects and takes us on a grand tour of his workmanship through several developments on the road. He is like a white-haired Easter Bunny, hopping from room to room, showing us marble, cornices, ceilings and period furniture pieces. His enthusiasm is contagious.

We are introduced to his sons who work for him. They have thick Irish accents, which is the only attractive thing about them. Tweedledee and Tweedledum. Tweedledee works hard for his father and is dull and serious. He does not get irony. Tweedledum does all he can to avoid work and smoke pot in his small basement flat. It is not decorated Edwardian style.

The grand finale of the tour is the penthouse suite. It is fully furnished, and every detail is exquisite. It is charmingly feminine in Marie-Antoinette pastels and plush finishes. A large antique gold mirror fills the space above the marble fireplace. Voluminous silk curtains, a pale shade of berry, billow in the breeze. The furniture is all Edwardian with modern, white wooden framework and soft mint upholstery. The four-seater couch is curved around the fireplace like a Persian cat languishing in the sun. The kitchen is fitted with every modern convenience. There is a large oval jet tub in the bathroom and two darling double bedrooms made for modern princesses. The best feature is a hatch and small ladder, which allows you to climb onto the rooftop and look across the watery grey skies and never-ending London rooftops, like the kings and queens of the castle.

We are smitten. It is a fairy tale of unicorns and rainbows. It is candy floss and satin sheets. It is macaroons, Turkish delight and bubbly pink champagne. It is white clouds and turtle doves. It is love at first sight. It is exquisitely opulent and outrageously expensive. The monthly rent could buy us a small car, but we know we can earn this in one or two nights.

It's perfect.

"We'll take it."

We sign on the dotted line.

It will make the most adorable boutique brothel.

We have now placed ourselves in a position in which we will have to work awfully hard to maintain our lavish lifestyle. We are in over our heads. We have committed ourselves to handing over £265 per week to the mad Easter Bunny (R5,258 per week today). But we are too taken up with our upgrade from downscale basements to our penthouse in the sky.

I can sleep off the sleaze in my Egyptian cotton sheets and swan around in my candy floss world, maintaining a thin but pretty veneer over the rotten, perverse and enslaving underworld I move so easily in and out of. I choose fantasy over reality and stuff my face with beautiful, delicious lies. "High-class call girl." What an oxymoron! We are not cheap. A date will cost £150, sex at least £300. In 2021, this equates to R8 000 and R16 000 respectively. Standard rates. Cash only. We are high-class, top drawer, cream of the crop, A-grade.

But I have it all back to front. In a society with clear-cut categories of class, how could a South African art degree dropout and a half-Scottish, half-Aussie girl possibly be anything but low class, lower working class at best? The label 'high-class' doesn't refer to us after all. It's the clients who pay for us who are 'high-class'. Like First Class seating on British Airways, it's the man who can afford the ticket who has the status, not the hostess serving the drinks. We are utterly insignificant, worthless, expendable and in servitude. We do not matter. Entitled men, even more entitled to objectify and use us the moment cash is handed over. Men who trade in stocks and flesh. Everything can be bought for the right price.

On Saturday mornings, after slumbering off our champagne hangovers, Sally and I usually take languid walks through the Oxford Street food market, our faces scrubbed squeaky clean and make-up-free, wearing faded jeans and ponytails. We gather gourmet eats for a Sunday feast with our dirty bank notes. We fill our basket with ripe strawberries, black cherries, butter-yellow cheeses, meats, ciabatta loaves and cured Italian meats.

We weave through the stalls, heckling red-faced traders and tasting the sea in mussels and crab meat. My hunger claws from inside, from a desire to taste goodness, wholesomeness and purity. As if by eating a golden delicious apple or homemade pork pie, I can nourish my soul and satisfy my yearning for something I ache for: home and lost innocence. I look for these elusive things in baskets of fresh fruit and the smell of salted fish, steaming tea and sweet jasmine honey. Tastes and aromas take me back to a place I cannot return to and yet I search hungrily, as if it could be bottled like apricot jam and eaten on warm bread. Doorstep slices of bread eaten with Maggie sitting on the stoep of my childhood home. All washed down with the comfort of sweet tea. Mixing cement.

Rows of dead silvery fish with lifeless eyes stare back at me from their beds of ice. I cannot look at fish bodies and not think of standing beside my dad at the edge of grassy dams and gently lapping water, my toes squishing into the mud, knowing it does not matter that I am a girl. I can do all the boy stuff just as well as any son. The delight of the tug at the end of the line and the flash of silver in the water as the freshwater bream is reeled in. Poking my finger into the jelly-like eye and squealing with feigned horror. Watching Dad gut the fish with his army knife, gagging and pinching my nose when the entrails spill out with a fishy stench. We'd look in the stomach for anything interesting, like a half-digested creature of sorts, almost expecting to find a trinket. Muddy wriggling worms or white bread rolled into balls for bait. Smokey fires roasting meat, relaxing in rusty camp chairs on the outskirts of town during a guerrilla war. All washed down with a cold beer and a glass of cheap white wine.

※

Life in our posh apartment settles into a routine of days and nights as different as light and dark, stitched loosely together and worn in with the familiarity of an old blanket. Groggy mornings, smudged eyes, suppressed loathing, late lunch leftovers, clean laundry, bathing, blow drying, charcoal eyeliner, high heels and snorting white powder confidence. Taxis, red lipstick, city lights, shimmering nights, champagne, sushi, swanky nightclubs, grey dawn light, wads of cash and dirty laundry. Suppressed loneliness. Wash, dry, repeat.

In the flotsam of this city, I am floating and drifting, unaware of the dangerous undertow and currents below the dark waters. I am swimming in murky water, with unknown enemies brushing my legs. I am floating in crocodile and hippo-infested water, where you cannot see your own limbs in the black shadows and your body can disappear out of sight in a cold moment. In this city there are dark shadows and hidden dangers we pretend not to see. We are young and beautiful. We are gazelles, unaware that there are lions crouching in the tall swaying grass. I am too comfortable with danger lurking just out of sight, with the Boogeyman at the window and the terrorist under my bed. I don't panic when I should. My mental and emotional alarm bells, rusty and worn, my ears and eyes dulled from a childhood peppered with raids, rifles, sirens and alarms.

Besides being anaesthetised to risk, I am barely out of girlhood and full of the worldly ignorance of the young and carefree. Even if I knew that a prostitute is two hundred times more likely to be murdered, I would somehow think I am immune to such peril. I don't understand I am low-hanging fruit. No one searches for runaways, drug addicts and dead hookers.

Even if I had come across news about the notorious 'Green River Killer', Gary Ridgway, I would not have paid any attention. He told police he was sure he could kill as many hookers as he wanted and would not be caught. He told them he thought he was doing them a favour. He murdered forty-eight women, burying them in clumps along his truck route as macabre below-ground milestones. I would never have imagined myself as the kind of girl who would fall victim to a serial killer. I was unassailable.

In London, a 19-year-old call girl was murdered in her Fulham flat. She was discovered by her flatmate who found her naked corpse. She had been bashed over the head with a blunt object and strangled. There was no sign of forced entry. There was a hundred-pound note left untouched on her bedside table. The killer was never found.

Even the murder of 'a privately educated city girl' who was leading a secret life as a high-class escort would not have alarmed me.

When I learned that a hooker was bludgeoned to death with a pestle on her birthday by a banker in a cocaine-fuelled attack, there was no part of me that thought, "It could be me."

I could be any one of those girls and countless others, found washed up on bleak stony shores with slit throats, bashed heads and bloated bodies.

CHAPTER 18

NEW YORK, NEW YORK
May '89

The Gecko wants to take me to New York! I have weighed up the pros and cons. Three days alone with him in exchange for a jet-set weekend in a five-star hotel and a shopping spree on Fifth Avenue. I decide to go. Since I am a British citizen, I foresee no problem leaving the UK. It is stamped clearly into my Zimbabwean passport.

The Gecko arrives to fetch me in his convertible. I am wearing my best Topshop outfit. It's a teeny turquoise miniskirt and a peasant-style blouse with a red cherry pattern, paired with cowboy boots. Looking at myself reflected in the shiny car door, I think a New York shopping spree may be a necessity rather than a luxury. My trashy outfit is no match for his Versace suit. I look like an extra on the set of *Footloose* and he looks like the Texas mafia.

At duty-free he buys me a new camera and a bottle of Chanel No 5. I am bubbling with excitement and the usual snooty stares roll off me like water off a duck's back. I stretch out my long bare legs and cross my cowboy boots, sip on champagne and eat caviar heaped onto melba toast.

We fly over the New York skyline at midnight. It is a universe of lights that takes my breath away. The city's pulsating energy and glittering skyscrapers thrust into the night, promising adventure. By the time we land and disembark after an eight-hour flight, I am tired and crumpled and dreaming of silk sheets, fluffy towels and a cup of tea. Nothing has prepared me for the rigours of American border security.

The airport officer looks at my Zimbabwe passport, looks back at me, looks at The Gecko and waves someone over. I say in my most convincing British citizen voice that I do not require a visa to visit America from England. It suddenly dawns on me that I have no money, no relatives, no idea of our hotel address, no visa, and an African passport. I feel very unwelcome. I am lacking in all the basic requirements for visiting the Land of the Brave and Free. My confidence melts under the harsh airport lights and puddles at my feet.

The Gecko tries to vouch for me and claims full responsibility for me. The officials are not impressed. I am starting to feel like a scantily dressed White refugee. White trash. I really should have dressed more modestly.

I am separated from Gecko and escorted to an interrogation room. Two border police enter and take out ominous-looking notepads and forms. I must make a statement. What are my motives for entering the US of A? What am I here for? What is the reason for my visit?

I cannot say, "I am here to have a sexy weekend with a smarmy rich Texan so he will take me on an expensive shopping spree, possibly some sight-seeing." All my attempts to explain are unconvincing. I am not easily intimidated but I am feeling like things are going very pear-shaped. I am trapped in a good immigration cop, bad immigration cop movie scene. The good cop brings me bitter coffee and appears to feel sorry for me. The bad cop tells me I am in serious trouble. Gecko and I have been separated and will be detained and questioned separately. They want to find holes and loops in our story.

Is this what it feels like to be a suspect in real life? I have no one to call for help. No one to vouch for me or rescue me. I am starting to understand what a mess I have got myself into, but I still don't understand my crime. Being dressed like a cheap hooker? Being a White South African? Being too young for my escort? The border police are completely immune to my charm, which has always got me out of sticky situations before. I want to confess but I still can't figure out exactly what I have done wrong.

I am questioned for two exhausting hours. I am sure this will all be over soon when they understand I am completely harmless, but my story and my Zimbabwean passport don't hold up under scrutiny and a big stamp is pounded into it, saying in letters of red rejection: DEPORTATION.

Gecko is on the other side. He is American so they can't reject him. I wave goodbye forlornly to my all-expenses-paid weekend as he turns around and disappears into the crowd.

I am police-escorted through the airport and taken to board the next flight back to London. It is humiliating being unceremoniously dumped in economy class and shipped back to where I came from. Dragged onto the plane like a stray cat by an officer, in full view of every passenger. I hope England will take me back. I am feeling very undesirable right now. I will be there by morning with the rush hour traffic.

Once on the plane I am squeezed between two plump and jovial British holidaymakers. I do everything to grumpily swat away any conversation or awkward questions. I will slap my neighbour if she tells me another chatty anecdote about New York. I tuck myself against the window and look wistfully at the flickering city lights mocking me from the sky. New York, New York. *If I can make it there, I'll make it anywhere.*

All I have to show for my trip to New York are my airport souvenirs, a camera and bottle of Chanel No 5. And a ticket stub.

A few weeks later, The Gecko visits and tells me it was the most nerve-racking two hours of his life. I am touched at his concern for my well-being.

"I was questioned and searched," he drawls. "I was worried they would find them. It would have been very unfortunate for both of us if they had. Mostly likely we would have been arrested. It was touch and go but I think you were a distraction, lucky for me!"

I wasn't feeling terribly lucky at all. I was still bleak at missing my Fifth Avenue shopping spree.

"They were in my briefcase, inside the lining and in my secret pocket." His slow Southern drawl is taking too long to get to the point.

"Find what?" I ask.

"Diamonds."

Stitched into the lining of his crocodile skin briefcase, were diamonds.

I should process the possible outcome if he had been caught but instead, I think of how geckos drop their own tails to escape danger. I picture The Gecko leaving his scaly appendage wriggling at the airport. I laugh it off as a narrow escape, just another adventure.

But the words "you were a distraction" can't be unheard.

CHAPTER 19

THE AMERICANS

May '89

At some point, in some club, on some night, bouncing off the walls on a cocaine-fuelled rampage, we befriend two male American underwear models. Stupidly handsome with names like Brad, Ridge, Chad or Chip – I can't remember – they remind me of big goofy Labradors, bounding with energy, eager to please and not very bright. We refer to them as 'The Americans' or 'The Boys'. They visit us in our apartment from time to time. We have an arrangement of sorts, an unspoken agreement between the four of us.

The things unspoken are they are too handsome to pay for sex and they know we are call girls. I suspect this is what makes us a sexual curiosity. There is no illusion between any of us that there is a possibility of a relationship or future of any kind. Curiosity, convenience and sex. A wild ride.

We'll say, "Let's invite The Boys over" when we feel like we need a break from middle-aged, balding, sagging desperation. They are our antidote to all the sad and sordid hours, a breath of fresh, young, firm, boisterous air.

Sally likes the younger one – blond, boyish, all-American wholesomeness, a real sweetheart. She is going to eat him alive. I pair up with the other one. He is in every way the tall, dark and handsome cliché. Wavy jet-black hair, concrete jaw and body. His sculptured features will make him look distinguished when he is much older, and his hair is peppered with silver. We have literally nothing to say to each other and show no interest in knowing anything personal about each other anyway. The relationship is pure in its total lack of pretence. All social foreplay has been discarded and we silently grant one another permission to be our most primal selves. A man and a woman. Nothing more.

I make him strip while I lie back on the curved couch and watch. I make him stand naked while my eyes wander over his body. He stands proudly, erect, filling the space with raw masculinity and aromatic testosterone. He smirks at my unmasked lust and appreciation of the physique he shows off. He is freakishly taut, rigid and hairless, like a statue.

Up close I can see tiny pink puckers like permanent goosebumps where unwanted dark hair has been waxed for underwear commercials. I want to treat him as I am treated, as an object, a slab of meat. I want him to be nothing more than the recipient of my hunger for the most basic form of human connection. I am in charge. I make him do what I want him to do to me. I am demanding, forceful, aggressive. I want to engulf him and swallow him and wrap myself around him, clinging to his brawny, unyielding strength. I claw and scratch him like a feral cat. I grind against him till I am raw and we are slick with sweat and I have pushed his endurance to its limit, till there is nothing left but exhaustion.

Sally and the other American stay in her bedroom, giggling and chatting like teenagers. We usually stay in the lounge but sometimes I like to take him to the rooftop and have sex in the cold dark air. I like watching our breath mist around us, his broad shoulders framed against the night. I don't care if anyone is watching. I want to feel the icy cold, our body heat, our hot breath, to feel naked and exposed, to feel alive.

I urge him to be rough, to hurt me. I want the pain and chilling exposure to explode together. I want to scream, and I do. I cannot muffle the carnal cry that surfaces from deep inside me where all my fractured parts are waging war and grasping to hold on to life. Howling like a she-wolf to the moon.

I avoid taking him to my room. My bed, my bedroom with its small wrought-iron balcony is a soft small island I can swim to. A four-walled haven in the mad melting chaos my life has become.

I've been sucked into a vortex, spinning around and around with no way up or down, like the fairground ride rotating so fast the centrifugal force leaves you glued to the wall. I wrap myself in my bed sheets and clutch my pillow, trying to hold fast onto something while the ground below me has completely vanished.

CHAPTER 20

WILD GOOSE CHASE

May '89

We had big dreams of making our penthouse suite our business boudoir, but instead we're stuck working in the gentleman's club. We have one problem we had not foreseen in our vision for establishing the classiest boutique brothel in London. Tweedledum is extremely inquisitive and bombards us with questions about our comings and goings at night. He is always stoned but it is still risky. His dad, the owner, is always around, working on his ongoing gentrification of the road. We cannot afford too much suspicious activity, or we will be reported to the police. We must be very discreet. For now, it's safer to carry on working in the club.

We do, however, have Gecko over regularly with cash and cocaine. Sally also has another private client friend who comes to see her here. They both like the 'two-in-one' deal we offer. Sally and I have no inhibitions with each other and know the men love being with both of us at the same time, it's the ultimate male fantasy. Blonde and brunette, girl-next-door and dark-eyed gypsy, slim and curvy, benign and quick-witted. Sandra Dee and Betty Rizzo.

Payment is less specific – cocaine, expensive dinners and some 'spending money' are left on the bedside table as tokens of appreciation for our sexual attentions.

Sally is more prone to the odd one-night stand; she likes bringing guys home from nightclubs and parties. I think she might be hoping to fall in love. I don't see the point. I need my alone time and my space. I am really annoyed when one night she drags home a playmate and he brings a friend along. Sally and her pick-up disappear. I am left to entertain the friend, who has assumed I am up for the same games his friend is playing in the other room. I am not. He is as dull as a doorstop, unattractive and won't leave me alone. I don't know how to get rid of him and try getting him drunker than he already is. Perhaps he will pass out. Instead, he gets pushy and lecherous. His red, slobbery face and leering is getting on my nerves. I need to ditch this jerk.

I suggest we play hide and seek and tell him to close his eyes. Catch me if you can. As soon as his back is turned, I go to the latch that opens the exit. I climb up the short steel ladder, through the hatch to the flat cement landing. I can hear him stumbling about below. I have a few moments to think of my next move and decide to lead him on a wild goose chase. I can hear him getting closer to the ladder and latch and I know that he will soon figure out how to get out.

I've only ever been on this small cement landing, but I look at the steeply pitched top of our apartment and make a split-second decision to climb onto the roof. I pull myself up onto the grey slate tiles and clamber up to the pointy ridge. My legs straddling either side of the roof, I scoot as far along the top of the ridge as I can in an odd leap-frog type movement. I am at the far side of the flat, above Sally's bedroom. I swing my legs over so that I am sitting perched on the penthouse roof, towering four storeys above the ground. He's reached the first landing above the kitchen but can't see me. I hear him calling out, breathless and confused.

I can't go back. I look down the slope of the gable. I can just see the white eaves, a thin ledge as narrow as a gymnast's balance beam. It's dizzying, precarious and one wrong move will have me splattered on the pavement.

Without hesitation I slide down the shale roof feet first. My body is pulsing with a heady mix of alcohol and adrenaline. Alcohol impairs judgement and inhibition. Adrenaline floods your body with energy, sending blood to the muscles in preparation for flight.

Whoosh.

Down I go and miraculously land my feet on the ledge, the only thing that's keeping my body from the ground below. I scoot along till I see Sally's bedroom window and the window ledge. Swinging myself over and dangling my legs over the roof, I manage to get a foothold on the ledge and finally, my arms can let go of the eaves, one by one. I am now attached to the outside of the window like a drunk monkey. Sally lets me in. I slip through the passage into my room and lock the door.

I go to sleep leaving the jerk on the roof wondering what happened to me. I've performed a vanishing act! The next time I walk on the pavement below our building and look up, I am horrified at how close to the hazardous edge my nocturnal escapade was. But I am accustomed to doing things without evaluating the risks first. I have an uncanny way of coming out unscathed.

How many times had I been drunk when driving my grandmother's beat-up Mazda? Once I was flying up the hill, totally inebriated on my way home in torrential rain. The car spun out of control, did a few 360 turns and skidded to a halt on the wrong side of the road. I got out, pulled the dented wheel hub off the tyre, got back in the car and carried on driving. Gran's car was already so banged up from her own mishaps reversing out of the driveway that no one ever bothered about another dent. I could always have blamed her if they did.

We were a family who camped in the remote wilderness of the Kalahari, in places where you had to take your own water, fuel and food. You would be dead in a matter of days if something went wrong. We had survived a civil war. Dad had taught me to drive in his vintage Toyota Land Cruiser. He had said, "If you can drive this, you can drive anything!" We drove around Cordwalles School, my two sisters squealing with terror in the back when we almost capsized. My dad is a natural born adventurer. Kalahari Keith. Tigerfish catcher. Survivalist. We were not raised in cotton wool. We did not have 'helicopter' parents. We were treated no differently than if we were boys. Dad adored being the hero to his gang of girls.

Before I left home, we went on a long family holiday. It was hardcore. No luxuries. Dad had made us practise putting up the tents every Sunday for months before the trip. It was like army bootcamp. We drove across Botswana, three girls in the back of the truck with only canvas flaps to protect us from the elements.

At the end of every day, we climbed out of the truck covered head-to-toe in grey, powder-fine dust like ashen ghosts, our cheeks stained with muddy streaks from our watery, bloodshot eyes. On our way to Chobe River, our final campsite, we came across a man with a broken-down truck and a boat. A man with a boat in the middle of the desert is unexpected. He was on his way to introduce parasailing to the Chobe River Guest Lodge. My dad offered to tow him and the boat.

To say thank you, he offered Dad a free parasail along the Chobe. It was untested, and he would be the first man in the history of the world to do so. My dad declined. He said there was no bladdy way.

The Chobe River is infested with crocodiles and hippos. Crocs are bad news, but hippos are even more dangerous, notorious for killing humans that get in their way.

Not wanting to seem ungracious, my dad instead volunteered his two elder daughters as guinea pigs. I am an experienced swimmer and waterskier, but my younger sister, not so much. The idea was firstly, to launch from the bank of the river on skis, as one could not wait in the water to be pulled by the boat. Secondly, the boat had to keep one steady in the air as it pulled you along, so that you did not get tangled in a tree or the swamps. Thirdly, you had to be followed by a second boat which had to get to you as quickly as possible. Every second in the water meant that you were live bait, dangling at the end of a large, deflated balloon. There was some speculation about whether the sound of the boat engines would be enough to scare off the crocs and hippos.

I went first. My skin prickled with goosebumps, my breath was knocked from my chest as I floated like a helium balloon above the delta. At seventeen, it was the most exhilarating and hair-raising thing I had ever done. My sister was not so lucky. The cords tangled, wrapping around her neck. Her flight was aborted and she had to be fished out of the river. She was traumatised. She was just thirteen years old.

CHAPTER 21

SCOTLAND

June '89

Sally and I need a break. We decide that we need to go on a holiday and we've been begging and cajoling The Gecko to pay for us to go on a road trip to Scotland. He's reluctant to fund a holiday which does not include him, but we wear him down with whining and pleading.

Finally, he agrees to hire us a car and give us some cash. I am excited to finally be doing some travelling. We pick out a red Ford Sierra convertible and are ready for a racy road adventure.

Sally was born in Scotland and knows her way around. She wants to visit a friend in Oban and from there we will take the ferry to Mull.

We decide to take our hamster with us on the trip, or she will die. We fell in love with the Russian miniature rodent when we spotted her in a pet shop window. We carried her down to the subway and decided to name her by asking the next pretty girl we saw what her name was. When the pretty girl we tapped on the shoulder told us her name, we knew it was perfect for a Russian hamster. Anastasia.

Our little hamster princess will be road tripping with us.

It feels so good to be out on the road, just driving away from the city, free to explore. I had not expected Scotland to capture my heart the way it has. The pristine beauty of the rolling hills, craggy mountains and glass-clear lakes is breathtaking. There is something else beneath the obvious beauty that reaches my soul. It is an ancient place, blood-soaked with history. A place of secrets and stories. A place of mystery and folklore. I feel a tug to its distant past, a place standing still, unmoved, unchanged, like the forest of a fairy tale. I long to be swept away into a living dream which seems possible now, driving through the misty landscapes. All that is dead and dull, numb and unresponsive in me starts thawing like a stream in the first days of spring.

We stay over with Sally's friend in the bay city of Oban. He adores Anastasia and we decide she must begin a new chapter in her life and remain with him. The next morning, we take our car on the ferry to the Isle of Mull. We check into a quaint guesthouse in Kilmore, where we have a bed and breakfast option. We plan to spend our days roaming around the island.

There is something about being on an island that makes me feel like the rest of the world has drifted away. Here, we are just two young, free-spirited girls on holiday.

We spend days exploring the rock pools and following worn paths along the rugged, weather-beaten coast. We drive along the narrow country roads looking at castle ruins and small villages.

Sally is quiet and withdrawn. I sense it is a place holding complicated memories for her. Her mother left her when she was young. She does not know her father. On one of our drives, we pass a lonely ramshackle cottage with a rundown caravan slumped in the backyard.

She says flatly, "That's my grandfather's house."

I am surprised, as she hasn't mentioned him before.

"Are we going to visit?"

Her eyes never leave the road, and she says coldly, "I'll never go back there."

It is then I know unspeakable things have happened in this desolate place. I feel sick to my stomach looking at the forsaken caravan, knowing that it holds a dark and shameful history.

I had not known how hungry I was for the outdoors. I run around the small beach alcoves like a giddy child, splashing in the icy water, clambering over rocks and peering into rock pools. The salty, fishy sea, the crunchy pebbled beaches and the wind whipping around me are like cold water to a parched throat. I can't get enough. I want to cling to the stones and the moss. Nature grounds me, helps me to find my balance and the girl inside of me. The wilderness child playing in the dirt, scraping her knees, collecting mermaid treasures along the shoreline.

We are going out for a night on the town. We dress up and drive down to Tobermory. It's a postcard-pretty place with brightly painted buildings lining the bay like maids in waiting. We go early to enjoy sundowners and to see the town before dark.

There are enough pubs along the main street to keep us entertained for the night. We end up in a bar full of rowdy locals and a pool table. Sally and I are pool sharks and love to hustle.

We leave with two guys we have been drinking and playing pool with all evening. We all drive off together, with no real plan in mind. We end up in some farmer's field sitting on the roof of our car, looking up at the stars.

I know how this is going to end and I just let it happen. It's just easier to give in. The fleeting moment of attention, of feeling wanted, even if by a stranger, will comfort me and plug a lonely hole, if only for a cold, drunken moment. I want to be held and kissed. It doesn't alarm me at all how easy it is to surrender my body to someone whose face I will not remember in the morning. I try to romanticise the scenario, two lonely souls under the starry sky, but I know it's just shallow and wretched.

We don't go back to the town again. I think we both knew it had tarnished our holiday. We had revisited hollow sexual encounters like dogs returning to their own vomit. We stick to the coast and the fields, away from any other humans. We sleep in our cosy quilt-covered beds, sit by the fire at night and are reluctant to leave the country's warmth and hospitality.

But we have a slight problem. We have no more money. It would not be too problematic if we had paid our hotel bill up front. We cannot check out as we can't pay the bill. We cannot stay and keep running up the account even further. We cannot flee in the night. We have no money for petrol. We also have no money for food.

We are high and dry in Scotland.

We have no choice but to stay put and figure out a plan. In the city, cash is on tap. On the Isle of Mull, we have no resources. We will have to try and reach out to The Gecko. This will involve finding a public call box somewhere on the island, trying to time it so that we get him and not his wife on the other end of the line. He will be furious. He will not be able to pay the bill directly as the hotel in Kilmore will show up on his credit card statement. He will have to wire us the money. This will take several days. In the meantime, we need to survive. We decide to live off the land.

Sally has wangled some fishing rods, a large bucket, matches and cooking pot from a local farmer. We scour the rocks for clams and mussels. We climb along the perilous rock-faced cliffs to fish. It feels like I am standing on the edge of the world looking out at nothing but the churning sea. Shivering and drenched in freezing salty sea water, we tangle our line in the rocks and lose our clam bait with nothing but cold blue hands and a few piddly mackerel to show for our efforts.

It's a gloriously happy day – the flimsy rod and marble-sized sinker a tenuous line to a lost childhood. We notice some large crabs crawling over the rocks and decide this is a better food source. We catch seven and fill the bucket with them. We gather some stones to create a fire pit and balance the pot of water on the stones to boil.

Once the water is boiling, we drop the crabs in, trying to ignore the hiss and bubbles as they cook to death. We sit at our campsite like gypsy urchins, smashing open the crabs with rocks and sucking out the white meat. It's fresh, salty and the best seafood I've ever eaten in my life.

We are finally able to leave. Gecko has bailed us out of our country house, and we head back, passing castle ruins and monuments to the dead. I feel a deep melancholy leaving a place I feel so much at home in.

CHAPTER 22

THE TOUR
June '89

Gecko is deeply concerned about our future. He does not see the irony in making full use of all our call-girl services while lecturing us on the dangers and limited prospects of our profession. His concern irritates me. It's not like I am planning to do this for the rest of my life. I don't take any of this too seriously. It's part of my adventure, a bit of fancy dress to play the naughty girl, the harlot. I plan to discard this life like a snake that sheds its skin and moves on. Close the door, close the chapter, climb out the rabbit hole and reinvent myself.

Gecko wants to rescue us and so decides to take us on a tour of London's sex trade to try and show us how dismal our futures will be.

We are dolled up for a night on the town with him. A night out with him is always a coke-fuelled, club-crawling bash. Sally and I coordinate our outfits for maximum effect. We both have wigs for extra va-va-voom! Blonde and brunette of course. My jet-black wig falls in ringlets down my back. My knock-out dress is white, made from ribbed stretchy fabric that shrinks to the size of an elongated sock when it's off and clings to every curve of my body when it's on. It is completely backless, long-sleeved and stops mid-thigh. I pair it with white knee-high cowboy boots. Sally wears something similar but in black. Blonde and black. Black and white. Sexy Siamese twins. We think we look ultra-glamorous and sophisticated.

The first stop is the glitziest club in London. It's a far cry from our quaint little black-door club tucked under the pavements. This is shiny bright, in your face, look at me ostentatious and very visible. The Gecko leads us in, one on each arm.

He always looks impressive, dressed head-to-toe in designer wear. He drips money and flash. We turn heads.

The interior is a large, sumptuous banquet hall. As you enter, there's a long, languishing bar all the way along the back wall. A third of the room has a few casual tables and chairs for cocktails. The rest of the room is a sunken dining area with plush seating around circular tables. It's huge, and packed to the brim with men and girls.

On the opposite side of the bar, towards the far end of the club, is a stage. A sexy cabaret performance is on the go, with a chorus of girls kicking their fishnet-stockinged legs up high. A small orchestra is playing live music. The room is black and gold.

We sit down for a drink. We aren't staying for dinner. Sally and I look around. There are beautiful, glamorous girls at all the tables, others waiting at the bar. Hostesses? Escorts? Companions for the night? There are no private booths, no secret rooms. Just dinner and a show. It seems innocuous. Sally and I excuse ourselves to go to the bathroom. We want to look around and watch what is really happening here. As we leave the powder room, an immaculately dressed Asian man approaches us. We chat discreetly to him and then re-join The Gecko. We've found out that the club operates covertly as an escort-type service, setting up girls with customers for drinks or dinner at the club or for business parties and dinners outside the club.

No one uses the word 'escort' or 'call girl'. They are hostesses or 'bottle' girls. Each girl is paid a hostess fee by the customer. She can get 'booked' to sit with customers several times during the night. A percentage of her hostess fees goes to the club, and she keeps the rest plus any tips. Her job is to keep the customers happy and spending money in the club, where the price of alcohol is massively inflated to rake in huge profits for the house. What she does when she leaves the club is her own business. Sex for money isn't openly discussed but if you agree to leave with the customer, a much bigger tip can be expected.

We called it The Chinese Club when we found out it was run by the Chinese Mafia. We go from one escort- and strip-club to the next, with our tour guide, Gecko, pointing out how each new place is a little less glamorous, ranking a little lower, than the one before. Each more tawdry and pitiful than the last, with the girls becoming marginally older and more jaded, tacky, with cheap wigs and bruised arms. Low class. Mostly all White Trash.

We are nonchalant and indifferent. The tour has only heightened my own vanity, puffed me up with pride. I feel pity for the fallen women but cannot see myself in any of them. They are far beneath me.

Our final stop, in the early hours of the morning, is a 24/7 dive. A small dingy pub with a single stripper. Inside, it's a squeeze to cram around a sticky table. Several barflies are hunched over drinks in the far corner. In the middle of the room stands a single pole with a frizzy-haired middle-aged woman hanging onto it. So, this is rock bottom, according to The Gecko.

She smiles broadly, baring nicotine-stained teeth when she sees us. She kicks a wobbly thigh in the air, does a teetering twirl and then saunters over to our table.

"Hello honey," she says to Gecko. "How are ye darlin'? Missed you!"

They catch up like long-lost pals. What is it with this guy? Does he trawl around the city collecting hookers like stray cats in an alleyway?

I know he wants us to be horrified by this sad lady stuck in her sad life. How long can she carry on stripping and serving her loyal hangers-on? There's no retirement plan for prostitutes. We feign shock and fill the taxi ride home with empty promises. I had seen the dark rings under her eyes, her belly bulging, her breasts sagging, the grey roots of her frizzy auburn hair, the utter hopelessness of a grubby pub full of sad sacks. I just couldn't see her as my future. It is incomprehensible. This will never happen to me.

My brain is still maturing. My prefrontal cortex is still developing, and until the myelin sheath is fully formed around my nerve fibres, my cognitive processes will be immature. Myelin, a layer of fatty acids and proteins around nerve cells, only fully forms in one's mid-twenties. It's like insulation tape for the electric wires in the brain and enables more complex brain processes, impulse control and the ability to understand consequences. My brain is literally not yet wired for risk management and long-term planning.

It's the scientific explanation for the Invincibility Complex of the young and reckless and is perhaps why, when approached by the immaculately dressed Asian man at the club owned by the Chinese mafia, we accept his offer to work there.

CHAPTER 23

THE CHINESE CLUB

July '89

Working at The Chinese Club is fast-paced. It is big and busy. I am just one of hundreds of girls who come and go. It's a big, decadent party, the embodiment of the greed, excess and opulence of the 80's in London. Sex, drugs and rock 'n roll. A coke-snorting, big-teased-hair, bright-eyeshadow, neon extravaganza. No one ever pauses in the 80's to ask, "Is this too much?" It's all about the too much. It's the decade birthing the "You can have it all!" mantra. We are the get-ahead generation. The step-on-heads and climb the corporate ladder era, in pursuit of the 80's gods of wealth and power.

The club is filled with crooked financiers, corporate kingpins and international high-flyers. I am swimming in a shark tank, and it's feeding time. The gentleman's club was a little pond of mostly harmless British elites. Now, in this cosmopolitan establishment, I am truly out in the big wide world. I have pushed my boat out into deep waters. I think I know what I am doing. I don't.

Back home in South Africa, everything is stifled by the puritanical and oppressive National Party regime. Everything is pushed underground, especially the truth. Anti-apartheid pressure is intensifying and international sanctions against apartheid have isolated the country, both culturally and economically. The country is unstable. Violence is escalating. It's chaos.

The ANC political party has led the charge to make the country ungovernable. Black on Black violence is widespread. Traitors to the party and informants working with the police are publicly executed in a brutal practice known as necklacing. A tyre is pulled over the traitor's neck and set alight, and he slowly burns to death, screaming in smoke and fire. But this is happening thousands of miles away from me.

My only reminder of South Africa's political turmoil is the permanent picket line outside South Africa House in Trafalgar Square.

Free Nelson Mandela.

CHAPTER 24

BLACK BEAR

July '89

The first time I have sex with a Black man I am paid £300.

We have spent the evening together at The Chinese Club, and I follow him back to his hotel suite. I hesitate slightly at the door, knowing I will cross into a place I cannot return from. The room is dark, with heavy mahogany furniture. A desk lamp glows in the corner.

My client is African American. He has a pleasant face, a larger than life personality with a deep booming voice. He laughs easily. He is in his late forties, about the same age as my father. A few grey hairs crown his temples.

He lies back on the bed like a well-fed grizzly bear and watches me. I undress slowly, carefully. I feel a strange anticipation, as if I have been waiting for this moment. To liberate myself from this final restraint, to unshackle this unseen chain tethering me to White purity, the last taboo.

I am aroused by this dark man. This forbidden fruit.

He is relaxed, waiting for me to initiate. I crawl onto the bed. I hurdle my leg over to straddle his reclining body.

I am here because I have set fire to my own morality and traitor's heart to embrace a life without virtue. I sit astride him. He is large. I submit to him, allowing him to enter the most hidden and tender part of my body.

As I put him inside me, I feel something in me giving way. A yielding. Something has broken. Afterwards, I lie beside him. He is chatty and tells me of his wife whom he loves and his children whom he adores.

I lie there thinking, "I just had sex with a Black man."

I feel ashamed it was so pleasurable.

CHAPTER 25

GREECE
July '89

Waking up in Athens with a view of the Parthenon from our hotel room window is surreal. I have been transported to the world of my dusty art history textbooks. The former temple, dedicated to the goddess Athena, sits on the Acropolis where it has been since the mid-5th Century, as if waiting for me to open the curtains and gasp at its glory.

Sally is indifferent. To her it's just another crumbling old ruin. I keep staring, as if it is a mirage that will vanish.

Gecko has flown us over for a week under the Mediterranean sun. We are taking full advantage of his desire to save us from our call-girl, club lifestyle and have been making all kinds of empty promises. "We really do want to be good girls and get our lives back on track." We convince him with our lies.

So, here we are. We have been flown to Athens to re-evaluate our choices and plan a better future. We will ferry across to Mykonos for a night and then fly to Paros to join Gecko for the rest of the holiday.

The day after we arrive, we go straight to a bustling hairdressing salon in the city. It is full of dark-haired noisy Greek women talking loudly over hairdryers. I pulled out my extensions before we left London and now need to rescue what is left of my own hair. We go out to dinner in a courtyard strung with lights. Traditional Greek instrumental music is playing. I am giddy with excitement. I am in Greece!

Gecko has already been in Greece for a week, staying on the island of Paros with his wife, nanny and two young children for a supposed family vacation. He has planned to spend his holiday juggling his wife, kids, nanny and his two call-girl mistresses on a small island. Things could get complicated. We are ready for mischief.

Mykonos is a blue and white daydream. The white walls are dazzling against the cobalt-blue-trimmed doors and shutters. It feels good to be out of grimy, grey London. At night, the island sparkles with lights, partygoers and music. It's intoxicating.

Two days later we are on a tiny plane headed for the island of Paros to serve as Gecko's secret playmates.

Paros is delightful. It's quaint, rustic and not as commercial as Mykonos. I am in love with the little village – the narrow, cobbled roads, the dry parched land, the pink bougainvillea creepers, the twisted grapevines and olive groves.

We head off for the local café to meet Gecko. He arrives red-faced in sandals and shorts, showing his skinny white legs. It's such unfamiliar garb for him, and I try not to burst out laughing. He is excited to see us and anticipates a week of dirty sex and sun. We, however, have planned a week of hide and seek.

He gives us the keys to the fisherman's cottage he has booked in the village. He has also arranged two Vespa scooters for us to get around the island and to be able to meet him at secret rendezvous.

We are instructed to completely ignore him if we see him with his family. We are burning with curiosity and can't wait to get a look at his wife. He'll pop around to our cottage to make clandestine plans to meet up. Sun, sea and scooters on a paradise island. What more could we want?

But I want romance and love, sunset picnics and walks along the beach with a handsome lover. I want Seth, not slippery Gecko, sunburnt and lascivious. I want giggles and long lingering kisses. Paradise is desolate without love.

When I allow myself to think of Seth or the possibility of romantic love, a pang of longing so sharp it catches my breath rips through me. I cannot afford to dwell on those tender thoughts, it is no longer possible territory. Any thoughts of the past or the future are treacherous. I need to stay in the 'right-now'. I need to keep my guard up. My only options are another meaningless fling with another stranger and keeping Gecko dishing out the cash. I feel apathetic and jaded.

We explore the town and beaches. Everyone tans and bathes topless. At first, I feel awkward taking my bikini top off at the beach. I am not usually uncomfortable being topless in the clubs but this is so open and public. South Africa is so conservative, but it's not a big deal here. No one cares.

When we are not on the beach, we walk through the narrow, cobbled streets of the village. We eat at sidewalk cafés and marvel at the sweetness of the tomatoes soaked in golden olive oil. An authentic Greek salad is simple, just chunky pieces of tomato and green pepper with a fat slice of creamy feta cheese. There is no lettuce. Everything drowns in olive oil. Crusty rustic bread, fresh garlic, black olives and more oil are served on the side.

The local inhabitants are mostly old and poor. Farmers and fishermen. The women seem ancient, dressed in black and wrinkled from squinting into the sun. The men sit in the cafés and play

Tavli, the ancient game which is the predecessor to Backgammon. Poverty has never looked so pretty. It is paradise for a tourist, but I sense life here can be harsh. The local people are hunched over working the fields or tending goats. I feel self-conscious in front of the gnarled old women, as if they can see my secrets and despise me for my tarty foolishness.

The freshness of the food, the purity of the salty air, the clarity of the sea water all feels jarring and disquieting. Its picturesque perfection feels too good to be true, a dream-like reminder of what is no longer possible.

I cannot muster the same feeling of freedom and joy I felt in the wilderness of Scotland. Perhaps it is knowing that Gecko and his clueless wife are nearby. It has cast an ugly shadow on the holiday, a reminder of the trade I have made to be here. I cannot flit about in a blue and white daydream. Instead, when I can, I get on the scooter and ride away from the pretty towns along lonely, barren, dusty roads to explore the more remote parts of the island. I ride till the sun sets and the chilly evening wind whips up around me. Away from the azure blue sea and sparkly white buildings, the land is stark, deserted and rocky. I belong here, in self-imposed exile. In no man's land. Alienated and barren-hearted.

※

We are driving Gecko crazy by constantly messing up arrangements, showing up at the wrong rendezvous and feigning disappointment that things are not going as planned. He is working himself into a frenzy, trying to juggle wifey and two mistresses on a small island. He is wildly jealous that we may find handsome Greek boys to play with. He reminds us he is not paying for us to have fun with someone else.

He needn't worry. There are no handsome Greek boys, just a few greasy-haired locals who try to follow us around. We are not interested. Gecko's obsession with seeing us but not getting caught is entertaining enough. He is totally paranoid and stressed. How is this supposed to be a relaxing holiday?

Seeing how terrified he is of his wife reveals a weakness we did not know existed in him until now. It is a grain of information, like a small irritant entering an oyster. The oyster's only defence is to secrete layer after layer of silky fluid over the foreign matter until a single pearl is formed.

This intrusion of a wife and family works its way into an idea, one we will embellish, layer upon layer until the pearly plot is formed. Our eyes have seen a gaping vulnerability, exposed and very exploitable. A chink in his designer armour.

It's possible that our plan started as a joke; an idea flung across a table while drinking chilled white wine. Who's to know who started it? Initially it was just an observation. Then it became a thought, that became a brainwave, that became a ruse, until it evolved into a fully-fledged blackmail scheme.

We do eventually see him and his family out one day. We are at a safe distance and watch them walking down the stone road towards the beach. His wife is dressed in a black kaftan and wears a wide-brimmed straw sun hat and large dark sunglasses. She looks in her thirties, her body showing the softening spread of having had two children. She is still attractive and looks intimidating, even from a distance. They look like any harassed English family on holiday with nanny, beach bags and kids in tow. No one would ever have suspected that he has his own little entourage spying on him from around the corner.

CHAPTER 26

THE STALLION
July '89

Back in London, we slip back into old routines. We circulate around a few different establishments but work predominantly at The Chinese Club. Sometimes I find myself in places, not knowing how I got there, just drifting along with a drunken crowd of men and girls like a stick swirling on a current.

Some nights I am at the club, some nights I escort with a group of business diners. Like the time I am sitting in a restaurant at a round table of six Oriental men and assorted girls. Are they Japanese or Chinese? I can't tell. The men can barely speak English, the girls are indifferent and none of us are here to make friends. We are just perks. We are part of the business trip to the city. Champagne and girls to celebrate a business deal.

I am no longer exploring, curious or intrigued. I know what is expected. I know what happens behind closed doors. I know what to do. I know what to say. I muster up enthusiasm and wind up the charm like a doll with a metal key in her back. Ha, ha, ha. I laugh at the pathetic jokes and the tired one-liners I have heard so many times before.

On the nights I am working, I smear my face with make-up. I dress the part. I snort enough white powder to keep my heart beating for the next few hours. I switch to autopilot. In this sleepwalking, half-awake state, whole hours and sometimes even entire days are lost.

I wake up unable to remember how I got home. I sleep for days. The fragments and flashes I remember are as shadowy as a dream, falling apart and dissolving as I reach out to touch it. I might be losing my mind, but I don't care, I like feeling numb. I like this drifting, empty, floating feeling. I am a spectator to my own life. I am glued to the spectacle, watching the impending crash in slow motion. Nothing can be done to stop the inevitable collision. Something was put into motion the day I went through the black door, down the rabbit hole, behind the velvet curtain. Tumbling down in the dark with nothing to grab onto.

How strange a thing I have become. How dark and devious.

In childhood games, I always wanted to be the witch, the wolf, the Red Indian. I wanted to be the other. I did not want to be the pretty princess, waiting longingly in a tower for the prince to come to the rescue. The princess is dull, insipid and not the boss of her own destiny. I wanted action. I wanted to be the instigator. I wanted to holler Red Indian war cries, beating my palms to my ululating lips and stomping my feet. I wanted to be the protagonist, not the hero. The bandit, not the sheriff. I feel a kinship to the villain, not the victim. I wanted to be the witch, screeching and keening, hunching my body and curling and twisting my fingers to make them crooked. I can do a bloodcurdling evil laugh that sends small children running in terror from the playground. I wanted to cast the spells and not lie in a glass coffin in the woods.

Well, here I am.

I have met a prince. Arabian. He has asked to take me out at The Chinese Club. He is arrogant enough to be royalty. He looks down his aquiline nose through dark, intense eyes. I have been told his status by someone in his entourage. I am supposed to be impressed but I am never sure if what I am told is true. This is a world of make-believe and lies.

He does carry himself well. He looks imperial in his ink-black suit and younger than most of the men I entertain. He's probably between thirty and thirty-five. I wonder why he is out with an escort. I am sure he could get himself a date. There must be dozens of beautiful young Arabian princesses lining up to marry him. I am surprised he wants me. I feel flattered. Arabs usually prefer blondes.

When we go out, he is considerate and very suave. It almost feels like a proper date. I have no romantic delusions but it's a small consolation to believe that a night of passion with a prince is possible.

I break two of my rules. I kiss him and I take him home to my bedroom.

To be totally honest, my rules have been loosely compiled and are often not strictly followed:

No kissing.

(Kissing is too intimate, too emotive. Kissing is for lovers, not customers. A kiss must be cherished and not handed out like after-dinner mints.)

No kinky sex.

(A bit of playful spanking and role-play is allowed. Nothing perverted. It's easy to keep this rule as most of the men just want to be with young girls. My youth is my prime commodity. I realise as you get older in this industry you must add to your offerings and seek out more deviant clients. It's the only way to compete against the young and nubile.)

Never let a client into my bedroom.

(My bedroom is sacred. It's for me to sleep in and escape to. It's not my place of work.)

Try not to be alone with someone in a place you don't know.

(Sally and I work together wherever possible. Luckily, a threesome is popular.)

I don't have a specific rule around money as talking about it is tacky. I rely heavily on a gentleman's agreement and generous tipping. There is an unspoken fee structure in the establishments I operate in. Minimum payment of £100 for hand relief, £150 for oral and £300 for intercourse. Double that for two of us. Dinner, drinks, hotel costs must be paid for. Cocaine is standard.

It soon becomes apparent why this prince would rather be with an escort than a date. He likes it rough. He is strong and wiry, full of taut energy like a caged stallion. I am just a body for him to pull and push and pound against, like a rag doll.

He shoves me onto my stomach and pulls my hips onto him. He yanks me and grabs my hair. I can hardly breathe. He thrusts into me. It feels like he might tear right through me. I understand this is what he needs from me. I accept his aggression in silence. It is savage but at least I feel something. I need the pain. The pain reminds me I am not dead.

It's a violent assault, a physical attack so flimsily guised as carnal passion that it's impossible to tell if a line has been crossed. It is sanctioned rape. It is what he paid for. I never said no.

It doesn't matter if you are a prince or a toad or a gecko. In this underworld society there is no Black or White, Chinese or Japanese, English or American. Skin is skin, flesh is flesh. What exists between us is a transaction. An agreement, an exchange. Nothing more. It does not matter if I am classy or trashy. It does not matter if the sheets are clean or dirty, the hotel expensive or cheap. It does not matter how courteous or considerate you are. It does not matter how much I appear to be interested in you, who you are or what you do. There is a transaction that completely corrupts any humanity and connection between us.

I trade my flesh. You pay for it. I know what I am offering you. I give myself to soothe your loneliness, your furtive fantasies, self-loathing and shame. I offer a fleeting moment of healing as you purge yourself on my body with glazed, empty eyes that do not see me. Night after night, I dance with a toad or a prince, a dance of quiet desperation, pretending neither of us will pay for this.

I pretend you are special, worthy of all my flattering attention. I pretend you don't repulse me. I pretend I don't pity your weakness and your neediness. You pretend you do not judge me or despise me.

My hungry eyes desire only your money, and I will scrub you off my skin before tomorrow. I throw my head back and laugh as bile claws my throat. I giggle when I want to gag. You will never know me because I change like a chameleon, a night-walking shape-shifter.

I am what you need me to be. A vessel for your rage, your lonely wretchedness and frustrations. I am here to surrender myself to your desires and bury my own in an unmarked grave. I go to places most will not dare go, like a nurse on the frontlines of war.

I mop up semen and stitch dismembered egos together with torn lace. The places I go to are not for the squeamish or faint-hearted. I need numb resolution and a sacrificial heart. There are things I cannot unsee or undo.

This is the dark territory of a man's weakness, his pathetic ego, his feeble wounds, his crippled will and his gaping lust. The humiliation of his urge. It is the belly of the beast. A place without heroes.

Love does not grow here. It cannot. There is no air for it to breathe.

I do not look for love anymore. I do not expect to find it. I cannot give my heart to anyone again. Who could love me?

Seth and I have kept in touch with a few letters and phone calls, but I still feel like I am always left dangling in the air, hanging at the end of the cordless phone. He did not try to stop me from leaving. He has not asked me to come back. There has been no grand gesture or confession of undying love. I would have given it all up for him.

I've offered him a sketchy idea of what I am doing here. He thinks I am a waitress who wears lingerie, a bit like a playboy bunny. I dodge any questions and when I do provide answers, I lie to him. I know I have burnt any bridge of going back to him and besides, I am stranded on the other side of the world. The damage is beyond repair.

I write long, tearful letters of confession, only to scrunch them up and throw them in the bin. There is no point. Only an idiot would think someone would come and rescue me. Besides, I am not a princess.

CHAPTER 27

PLAN B

August '89

Gecko is right. I need to plan for my future.

I have two ideas. Firstly, I am going to learn to type and take a desktop publishing course. Secondly, Sally and I are going to blackmail Gecko.

Learning to type is tedious. I sit with headphones on and look at a screen and plonk the letters appearing in front of me, or type what is being dictated to me through the headphones. The keyboard of the typewriter is covered so I cannot look at the keys. I am learning to touch type, which means I can type by touch and not by sight. It is like learning another language. Braille or sign language. Slow and painful.

At the end of the three-week-long course, which is free to anyone registered as unemployed, I can type thirty-eight words a minute. The finished page looks like I was trying to type while someone was shooting a pellet gun at my toes. Riddled with mistakes. Why are electric typewriters so sensitive to touch? I press 'f' and get 'ffffffff'. There is no backspace or delete on a typewriter. I stop and carefully paint out the mistakes with Tipp-Ex or white tape. I am hopeless and stand no chance of landing a decent secretarial job where the minimum requirement is 120 faultless words per minute. Never mind, I will do the DTP course and, with my artistic talents, maybe I can find work in a smart advertising agency.

The course is hosted in a community centre in Brixton. It does not look like the kind of place that produces high-flying advertising candidates. The motley group of unemployed misfits doing the course dwindles down after the first day to about five students.

After three days I have a certificate. I hope it will create opportunities for me. I still have no idea what desktop publishing entails or how to design a brochure on a desktop computer. Computers make no sense to me. The cursor blips on the screen waiting instructions that I can't remember. Is it control, alt delete or alt, F1 control? It's yet another language to learn. Still, I try to be optimistic – it's not a degree but at least I have completed something. I have a certificate.

But in the end, blackmail will be my big ticket out of here. My big score before I get out of Dodge City. My one last fling before I ride into the sunset of new possibilities.

Sally and I discuss our devious plans at length. We sit in Chinese restaurants, hunched over Peking duck, scheming and plotting. Chinese food is our favourite indulgence. Any extra cash we have is always spent on huge feasts of Chinese. My guilty pleasures are the tiny, square prawn and sesame toasts and the nests of fried seaweed. Crispy, bitter and salty. We read our fortunes in the cookies and feel optimistic when good fortune is promised.

We have weighed up the pros and cons of our blackmail plan and decide to go ahead with it. We will lose Gecko as a benefactor, but we will be rich. We will not have to work in any of the clubs again. I can return home to South Africa, proving to everyone I made it on my own, and show my parents that going to London was not the biggest mistake of my life, that I am not a drop-out loser.

The amount of money to extort is crucial, not too little – after all, we will need to share it – and not an unrealistic amount. We imagine Gecko would comfortably hand over £15,000. His holiday to Greece would have cost much more. We have come up with a genius way to set the whole con in motion and are mightily impressed with our cleverness.

Our mastermind plan is as follows: one of us will try and get Gecko alone, she will 'warn' him the other one is planning to blackmail him. In this way, we can test out his response and one of us will still be considered a 'good' girl. We are very sure that Gecko does not want his wife to know about us, or the other mistress that Sally says he's been seeing.

We have his home phone number. We will threaten to make a call to his wife and spill all his dirty secrets. This should be enough to pull off a lucrative fee for our silence. We are sure we can manipulate a nice sum of money with our genius ploy.

In the meantime, I am still determined to get a day job and make a decent living. I manage to find something at an all-female financial services company called Acorn Financial Planning. It sounds promising. Plenty of room for growth. It's a sales position. I have no sales experience, but I am a quick learner. How hard can it be?

It is extremely hard. I am part of a sales team, with a team leader. We are selling a financial savings and investment plan aimed at helping women set up a nest egg for their future. My job is to sift through surveys women have filled out and follow up on the leads. I then sit on the phone for hours, making calls to my list of leads and trying to set up appointments. I have a script to follow. There are whiteboards on the walls tracking our teams' targets. I will earn commission for each policy I sign up.

The entire sales pitch revolves around the concept of 'fritter' money. The unnoticed pennies people have 'frittered' away each month. These lost and unmissable funds can be redirected to a future goal, such as a holiday on a Greek island, a deposit on a car, or your child's education. There is a carefully constructed questionnaire with space to draw diagrams for the potential client. The goal of the appointment is to identify the frittered monies, the bits left after all expenses are paid, which are usually unaccounted for or simply wasted.

I do not have a financial policy. How much money have I frittered away, I wonder? How much money have I wasted on tiny, expensive prawn and sesame toasts alone?

I work diligently on my telesales calls and prospects. My team leader says I have potential. I show up for work, exhausted but determined. I keep working at the clubs to support myself and pay the rent. I have no choice until my sales commission starts flowing.

I get home most days in the early hours of the morning, sometimes as late at 3am or 4am. I sleep for a few hours and then get up for my day job. I function robotically, pushing myself to keep moving forward, to persevere. This is my way out of the sleaze, the exhaustion, the hole I have fallen and tumbled too far down into.

※

After weeks in this zombie state, I finally have an actual appointment with a potential client. She is young, early twenties. She's in a dead-end job and fully engaged in the process of identifying her 'fritter' money. She would love to save for a trip to a Greek island. She has £25 of money going down the drain each month. I think I have one in the bag! After me paying for our lunch at McDonald's, she says she needs to think about it. My enthusiasm crashes to the floor. I won't hear from her again, she will avoid my calls and make excuses not to speak to me.

At the end of the month, I sit in a roomful of Acorn salesgirls and their team leaders for our regional sales meeting. All the top sales reps are rewarded, and everyone claps. Samantha is the top sales lady again. She is in her late thirties and flounces up to the stage in her Calvin Klein jeans and crisp white linen shirt. She says her winning tactic is to give her clients a nice bottle of wine. Why didn't I think of that? She possesses a confidence that would make me sign on the dotted line and start my Acorn nest egg. I am trying to stay positive but my plans to earn my way out of my seedy night job look bleak. Who would take financial advice from a foreign, twenty-year-old working call girl? I still haven't made a single sale.

※

Of all the things to be valued and cherished, hope must surely be held dear and preserved at all costs. Hope must be protected, guarded and clung to like a lifeboat in a stormy sea. To lose hope is to die before the heart stops beating and the blood no longer runs through the veins. All things can be lost, but not hope. Even a fragile whisper of hope is better than no hope at all. When hope is snuffed out, only darkness and despair can fill its void.

I feel hope slipping away. I can no longer see a brighter future. All I can see is a trail of bad choices dragging along behind me like a snare of tangled fishing line, hooks and rusty sinkers. I am in a quagmire. I am stuck. I cannot go back, nothing can be erased or undone. I cannot move forward. I have reached a dead end, an impasse.

As a child playing along muddy banks and in sandy bush land, I used to be afraid that I would get stuck in quicksand, slowly swallowed whole until only my hand reached out above the ground. Struggling only hastens death by suffocation in thick, waterlogged muck.

Now, I've wandered into a swampy wasteland and struggling is futile. I am resigned to my situation. I have no choice. What is done is done. No turning back. I armour up again with my devil-may-care attitude and burn-the-world-down motto. If I am going to throw my life away, then let all hell break loose. I'll go down in flames. Watch me burn like a witch at the stake.

I am taking bigger risks. I am breaking my own rules. I go alone to places I am unfamiliar with, leaving on the arms of men I have met at bars that turn a blind eye to escorts. Danger and I skip along the grubby pavements arm in arm. We are childhood friends.

I think I can sift out the harmless pleasure seekers from those with dead eyes and hard hands. Those who look through you to their own rage and inadequacy. Sometimes I get it wrong.

Tonight I am in an apartment in an unfamiliar part of London. I am feeling very uneasy. My instinct tells me to get out and get away as fast as I can. This is not a harmless reveller. There is a black coldness in his eyes, and he looks through me without seeing me. He is a python. He will slowly coil around me and crush my bones. I've done what he is paying me to do but he wants me to stay longer. He is pushy, drunk and belligerent.

I need to leave as fast as possible without giving away the acrid smell of my fear. I dress quickly, then edge towards the door. I make excuses about needing to be up early and slip out before he can argue.

I leave without looking back. I hold my breath as the lift comes, afraid I will be yanked back to the room. I have no cash for a taxi and don't know where I am or how to get home. Everything feels like slow motion, it takes forever to get down to the ground floor and out the lift. I watch myself from a distance as if I am the victim in a horror movie. Get out! I follow myself with my own eyes, watching anxiously as I walk across the lobby in the hour of secrets. I have morphed into two people. One who has things done to her and one who looks away; one who walks, one who follows.

The doorman's eyes also track me. He knows what I am, and I know he knows, and this understanding passes between us even though I avoid eye contact. I clutch my coat around me, trying to hold in my shame, but it leaks out, dripping a trail of everything that is slowly disintegrating within me.

I walk down empty streets, listening for following footsteps, but I am alone in the city and there is no one who cares if I reach home safely. It's just me with my thoughts gnawing at my heels, following me like a mongrel dog hoping for some attention.

I cannot feed the mongrel dog; its appetite cannot be satisfied and it will feed on me till I am empty and devoured. I must keep moving and not stop to think. I keep turning into another street, looking for clues to lead me back to where I came from, but each turn only takes me to a street that looks identical to the one before.

I can't get back. I don't know the way.

How do I rewind the clock to a time and place before this? How do I find the me before this me? How do I undo what I have done and untangle all the knots twisting in my gut? It is impossible. I won't ever find my way back.

I eventually stumble into a street with a twenty-four-seven corner shop and an entrance to a tube station. Finally, something familiar. I wait for the early morning train, stone cold sober, while busy morning commuters bustle around me. I rub my make-up-blackened eyes, longing for sleep to erase the night. To erase me.

CHAPTER 28

CROCODILE
August '89

I still go to work every day at Acorn Financial Services. Financially, it's pointless but I like the girls, I like belonging to a team. I like pretending my life is normal. I am also too proud to quit and acknowledge my complete failure at a sales job. Is selling myself my only option?

Sally and I have half-heartedly discussed our blackmail plans, but I am distracted with long working hours, and we hardly see each other. When I am at the flat, I am too tired to do anything but sleep. We have been in the doldrums, passing like ships in the night.

But now it's Saturday and we are going out together. We are going to try a new venue that Sally has heard about. I am trying to muster some of the old sparkle, the mindless fun of getting dolled up. We are trying to feel good vibes, get the buzz going. The effort needed to summon enthusiasm is impossible without cocaine and alcohol. Sip and snort. Sip and snort.

The bar lounge we find ourselves in is modern, flashy and

upmarket. It is more Yuppie than upper crust. Glass doors on all sides of the bar open onto wrap-around verandas looking over the busy streets full of Saturday night partygoers. The drinks are expensive. There are shiny metal cocktail tables and stools dotted around the room. Loud music thumps in the background.

This is not an escort club. We are not employed by the bar. We are free agents, so we must be subtle in our quest to find customers. If I am caught, I will be thrown out or arrested.

It's a perilous game of Q&A to weed out the casual drinkers from those who have come with wads of cash and can be propositioned. I look around. First, eliminate all the men under the age of 35 – they won't pay. Then men in groups, they are here for a drink before heading to a club to pick up girls.

I scan the room for men over forty, on their own. I look for expensive watches, expensive suits, expensive shoes. I make eye contact and smile. I wait like a panther in the grass, ready to pounce when the prey is close enough.

Here he comes. He is rugged, rough-looking, like a mobster character. His face is scarred, but in the dimmed bar light I can't tell if it's from acne or something else. He is stocky, well dressed, obnoxiously confident. I've found a mark.

The banter between us is good, even though he is very full of himself and brags about how notorious he is. He is offended I do not know who he is. I can tell he is impressed I can hold an intelligent conversation with him and am not intimidated by his supposed notoriety. He is agitated and restless, but I don't pay much attention to it; he's just a typical coke-fiend.

At midnight, he says he has a favour to ask me.

I say, "It'll cost you."

He replies, "Don't worry Doll, I'll make it very worthwhile for you."

He explains that his driver's license has been suspended and he has an important errand to run. Can I drive for him? Sure, why not?

He takes me down to the basement where the car is parked. It's a midnight-blue Jaguar, sleek and shiny, it looks like it's worth a million pounds. I can't wait to drive it. The interior is unimaginably luxurious. Black leather seats, impenetrable tinted windows, as many buttons and lights on the dashboard as a small aircraft. It purrs as we exit the car park and head out towards the highway. It's a beast – silent, stealthy, powerful. I feel exhilarated, cruising down the M4 under the moonless sky.

Something in his mood has shifted. He is growing more agitated and restless. He directs me through a maze of streets, cursing if I make a wrong turn or if he can't remember the way. I start to wonder if this was a bad idea. I feel uneasy. This joyride is no longer fun, but there's not much I can do now. I will just have to stay calm.

He then says something that makes the blood drain from my body.

"Guess what, Bitch? I have AIDS ... and I am going to give it to you."

I have walked straight into a trap.

AIDS. A disease I am aware of as being rife amongst gay men and drug addicts who share dirty needles, but which has slowly been working its way into mainstream paranoia. Once a far-flung scourge in places like San Francisco and Philadelphia, it has now crept in through the back door and onto 'normal' people's lists of things to fear. It is now top of my list of things to be terrified of.

Safe sex used to mean sex during which I would not be beaten up or murdered. Safe sex was sex after which I would reach home unharmed. Safe sex did not make me pregnant or give me a nasty itch. Now, safe sex has become sex during which a deadly disease is not silently shared.

How could this terrifying, incurable virus have made its way into this moment, this car, with this pock-marked madman?

I try to keep it light and pretend he is only joking. Every part of me knows I am wrong. I've walked into shallow water where a scaly crocodile has been lying in wait. Lying so still, I did not see him till it was too late. Waiting to pull me under water and twist round and round till I have lost my sense of direction and cannot see my way out. Waiting to lock his jaws onto my torso and drag me down into deep, murky water to drown.

We arrive at a house, on a road I do not know, in an area I am not familiar with. He gets out the car and bangs on the front door. He is shouting. His rage is growing. I think, he must be stopping for drugs – it would explain his mounting aggression and paranoia.

I wait in the car, anxiously hoping he will get what it is he is looking for. Every door and dark window on the street remain tightly shut. There is not a soul in sight, not a murmur. Not a light goes on. Nothing.

I think, this is what 'the dead of the night' means. No sign of life. Nothing stirs. I am still telling myself everything will be okay, no need to panic, just stay calm, but I've seen something inside him snap and I know I will not be able to reason with him.

He returns to the car, furious, spitting venom, his eyes black with rage. He tells me to get into the passenger seat so he can drive. I do exactly as he says. He drives further down the road into darker shadows, turns the car off and presses a button, locking all the doors.

He thrashes about wildly until he finds what he is looking for under the car seats. A switchblade. Click. The knife flicks open. The blade is thin, dull silver. My brain tells me I am in real danger now, but my body cannot react. I am here, but I am not here. I have shifted gears and turned off any emotional response. I shut down and numb out, unable to function.

Even if I manage to get out the car and run, he will follow me. Who will come if I cry out or scream? No one will open the doors if I bang on them. All I can do is be what he needs me to be in this moment, shape-shift to be the vessel for his black rage. If I can do this, I may make it out alive. I have no experience dealing with a paranoid, psychotic coke-fiend with an AIDS vendetta.

What does he want?

He wants to kill me! He wants to infect me with AIDS. He wants to slit my throat. He wants to fuck me up. I know this because he is now screaming these threats and hurling abuse at me.

"Fucking CUNT....whore...bitch!

I will KILL you!

BITCH!

Useless WHORE!

Scream and I will CUT you!

I'll shove this knife up your CUNT, bitch!"

His eyes are popping out of his head, spittle dribbles down the side of his mouth. The car has steamed up. It's hot inside.

I feel my back, wet with sweat, stick to the leather seats. I reach slowly and carefully for my bag. He is delirious, his face contorted with rage. He doesn't notice as I grope around in the dark, reaching into my bag on the floor by my feet. My fingers are searching for the only thing that matters right now.

The only thing between me and death.

A condom.

I only have one.

Will it be enough to keep me safe?

My gut tells me I must not plead for my life, or any kind of mercy.

I must not offer sympathy or consolation to him. I must not show any kind of weakness or fear. He does not want my pity. I will do exactly what he tells me to do.

The only thing that matters seems utterly impossible. I. Need. Him. To. Wear. A. Condom. All my energy, focus and attention hone in on this one singular task. Nothing else matters. It becomes my sole preoccupation.

I look at the digital clock on the car. It flashes 2am. I have been in this monstrous game of cat and mouse for two hours.

Cats play with their prey. They drag out the kill, taunting and badgering the injured bird or mouse until it can no longer escape or retaliate. It's a tactic to tire out their prey and make sure it cannot defend itself against them with a dangerous bite or scratch.

I am worn out. I have no fight left in me. I've been toyed with and tortured like a broken bird. I've been made to suck and fuck and had the knife at my throat, between my legs, in my face.

All I have tried to do is persuade him to wear a condom. He won't. He can't hold his erection for long enough and the condom is now sitting on the dashboard, crumpled and deflated.

He launches into a tirade again.

"FUCKING WHORE. BITCH. CUNT. STUPID FUCK-ING CUNT."

Menacing, contemptuous ranting. Most of it is incoherent, paranoid, indecipherable. I look at the clock. 3am. He switches the engine on. We drive to another location. He reminds me again that he is going to kill me. As if I have forgotten the murderous threats he's been screaming at me for the past few hours.

The words he's been hurling and spitting at me have seeped under my skin and burrowed down into the marrow of my bones. They pump through my blood and into every defiled organ of my rotting body.

They are true. I am a filthy whore. I am a fucking cunt. I am worthless.

There is nothing left in me that can defend or ignore this truth. In this moment, in this living, waking nightmare, I am everything he is accusing me of. I cannot fight back, I cannot escape, I cannot run, I cannot hide. I am nothing. I am nobody.

I am someone who can be discarded like the wasted, flaccid condom, shrivelled on the dashboard.

I am getting what I deserve.

This is the ugly truth.

We speak of the truth as ugly, brutal, dark and savage. Lies are beautiful and white.

There are no beautiful lies left to tell.

I cannot tell myself, "It will all work out fine," or "It's what you do, not who you are," or "You can leave this all behind you when you go back home." No, the truth is ugly. It's grotesque. It's almost too monstrous to look at. It stares me in the face. I stare back at it with unblinking eyes.

I am dirty White Trash.

I am unclean, revolting, feeding like a bloodthirsty zombie on white lies. I deserve to be punished, to suffer torment, to die lost and alone at the hands of a raving madman. I have sold my soul to the devil, and he has come to claim me.

I look at the clock. 4am.

We are driving again. He lied. He did not need a driver; he was looking for a victim. We drive for another fifteen minutes. He is more subdued. Or is he more resolute?

I am exhausted from trying to read him and be the perfect victim. I have surrendered limply to my fate. I don't care what happens to me anymore.

We turn down a narrow road. I notice the oak trees lining the street. The leaves are turning every shade of orange, they will drift to the ground and disintegrate, reclaimed by the damp earth.

We turn again onto a ramp sloping down to a double-garage basement. We are off the road, underground. Out of sight. The garage is white, lit with fluorescent light. The perfect place for an execution.

Has anyone died in here before, I wonder? Will he slit my throat or strangle me? Will he smash my head against the wall? I can picture the walls splattered with blood.

I have seen white walls dripping and smeared with blood before.

※

Our Grade Three school outing was to the local abattoir, to see how cows are slaughtered, dismembered and divided into quarters, and how portions will eventually be sold as slices of tongue, silverside and pink polony. I had thought 'tongue' was a name like 'salami' and not an actual cow's tongue.

Chinhoyi is a farming town surrounded by farms and farming industry. It should be no surprise we would be educated as to where our braai steaks and Sunday beef roasts come from. Our butcher always gave me free slices of polony, which I folded into quarters and bit holes into to make a polony-doily before I ate it. Sometimes I would put it on my face like a mask and stick my tongue through the hole at my little sister.

The other classes were lucky. They went to the cheese factory and the Willards crisps factory. They were given triangles of cheese wrapped in foil, and small packets of crisps.

My mother was horrified when I told her about the abattoir outing years later. She had no idea. There were no permission slips or indemnity forms for parents to sign. They had bigger things to worry about, like whether their husbands and sons would be killed while on army call-up.

I stand right next to the man in the white coat, holding the gun that looks like a huge stapler. He explains the cow will be shot between its eyes and this will stun it. It will not feel anything, it will not know where it is. It will be quick and painless.

Only a few of us at a time are allowed into the first chamber. From here we can watch the cow being stunned and then slaughtered. I eagerly push through the thick sheets of plastic and stand ready to watch.

The room is white and bright with fluorescent lighting. The floor is white, the walls are covered in white tiles. There is a steel basin with a long hose in the corner. A thick chain with a hook the size of a child's head hangs from a steel pulley. The men wear white coats with white plastic aprons and white gumboots. Everywhere is white.

Until it is not.

In the next few seconds that flash past so fast, the cow is prodded into the end of the funnel and the gate is closed, trapping it. The cow is shot between the eyes with the stun gun. The cow is jerked up on a chain. The cow is upside down, swaying to and fro from the chain. The cow's eyes are bulging wide with terror. The cow's throat is slit. The cow is twitching and jerking.

Blood gushes red and pure and dark. Blood mixes with water as it is hosed down. It pools and swirls in shades of pink and crimson as it is flushed down the drain.

It all happens so fast I almost feel cheated. I am moved along so the rest of the class can see another cow get shot with the stun gun. It doesn't feel a thing, we are told.

Next, we are ushered up a steel staircase to a landing overlooking the entire abattoir where we have a perfect view of the skinning, beheading, disembowelling, amputation and dismantling of the carcass.

The cow carcasses move along the production line until every part of them has been stripped and placed in steel trays and passed along the assembly line. Innards, eyeballs, tongues and tails trundle along the conveyor belt.

The stench from the macerated stomach contents is foul and overpowers the metallic smell of blood and the smell of fresh meat. The machines cutting through bone and sinew grind and screech.

I cannot see anything that looks like a sausage or a braai chop or polony. We are shuttled along to other parts of the meat factory and complete our tour in the place where the hooves end up. They will be ground into powder that will be used to make glue.

Our tour guide is enthusiastically explaining that nothing is wasted. Every part is used, not just for food, but for all kinds of by-products. The cow at least has sacrificed itself for humanity.

Here I am like a cow sent to the slaughter, in the empty white basement. We sit in silence in the parked car. I stay frozen, stare ahead but see nothing. I am weary to the bone. I cannot think or move. I can barely blink. I am still on a knife-edge, not knowing what will come next.

He is strangely subdued. I can only hope his drug-fuelled psychotic tirades have subsided. He looks as deflated and crumpled as the condom that is still stuck on the dashboard. He seems surprised that I am still there with him. He starts the car again and says he will take me home. We drive out onto the road like a ship that has weathered a battering and violent storm. The only way I can get home is to tell him where I live.

Night is lifting and the pink light of dawn is starting to show as he pulls the car up to the entrance to my apartment. His last words to me are, "I know where you live, if you tell anyone about this or go to the police, I will SLIT YOUR THROAT."

I get out the car. My knees want to buckle under the weight of the last five hours. When I reach the pavement, he winds down the window and throws a few hundred-pound notes onto the ground and drives away.

CHAPTER 29

LOST

August '89

It feels like the lowest I have ever stooped. Scraping that money off the pavement, picking up those dirty hundred-pound notes, destroyed what was left of my tattered integrity and bruised self-worth. I knew in that moment that I was every filthy word he had spat at me.

I drag myself up the two flights of stairs to the penthouse and crawl into bed. I sleep in restless sweaty fits. I try to curl into a ball to make myself as small as possible. I am lucky to be alive.

I don't feel lucky. I stay in my room. I avoid Sally. I don't want to talk about what happened. I cannot find the words for small talk.

I try to feel angry and vengeful. I can't. I try to feel sad. I try to feel pain. I can't. I lie in the bed, catatonic. My body is leaden. If I am thrown into a river, I will sink to the bottom without making any attempt to swim. My limbs will not flail, my legs will not kick. Water will fill my mouth and my lungs. My eyes will be dead and unblinking. I will sink to the bottom and lie lifeless in a watery netherworld.

My mouth is dry, but I can't drink. I drift between wakefulness and shallow sleep, jerking awake and gasping for breath. I know somewhere, far out of reach in the back of my mind, I have survived trauma. This knowing is trapped in a place that will not let the thoughts rise to the surface.

I know the term 'rape', but I cannot reach for the word. It falls through the cracks in the pavement where the money lay. How can a prostitute be raped? Even if he had not threatened me, I cannot go to the police. I cannot answer the questions I will be asked. I cannot be in a room with white fluorescent lights.

I must have phoned work and excused myself to my team leader. I cannot bear to have her ask if I am okay. Any kindness will feel like liquid acid on a raw, gaping wound. It will undo me completely. One question will pull loose a thread and I will unravel until I am just a pile of tangled wool on the floor. I will not know how to rearrange myself again.

I need to pull myself together. I can't afford to have a meltdown. I need to get through this. I don't know how to. I cannot deceive myself any longer, but the truth is treacherous. I am lost in a landscape littered with mines and booby traps. One wrong move. One wrong step. There is a war raging inside me, the lines have been drawn. Lies or truth? Hide or cry for help?

Truth keeps insisting, taunting and pushing through enemy lines. It is relentless.

WHORE. TRASH. WORTHLESS. PROSTITUTE. WHITE TRASH. This is what I am.

The lie that cannot hold itself up against the onslaught of honesty is the one that holds all the others chained along behind it. This is the lie – "I am not what I do," and "I can act like an escort, but not actually be one." Foolishly, I have believed my actions are outside of my innermost being, separated and detachable, like prosthetic limbs.

I have constantly told myself that I can walk away and leave this call-girl life behind. It will not follow me home. I can leave the trashy white dress, the knee-high hooker boots, the polka-dot brassier and all my shameful deeds here. I can pack my suitcase with my good girl belongings and the socially acceptable gap-year memories. Just leave the rest abandoned and discarded, in the trash along with all the used condoms. I can tell my wild adventure stories and leave out the sordid details. I can go back to life before this. I can pick up where I left off ... free-spirited art student.

The truth has me by the throat. It won't let go. I am what I have done. I cannot discard it like a gecko's tail, wriggling helplessly while the rest of me escapes harm. I am not unharmed. I am damaged goods. I am maimed and mangled and mutilated. I am defiled. I can NEVER go back to the me before this. I cannot pick up my life as if the last few months did not happen. I have set fire to my future, and it cannot be rescued.

I am in a barren wasteland. I walk around like the living dead, dog-tired and detached. I want to eradicate everything. I long for a black hole to sink into. I want nothingness, non-being, annihilation.

At night I stand on my balcony and look down to the cement below. Would the fall be enough to kill me, or just smash my bones? I would need to fall head-first and make sure I broke my neck.

CHAPTER 30

MY FUTURE SELF

September '89

I have reached a dead end. My life is a dead end. Is suicide my only way out of this self-made purgatory? Bare-bones survival or suicide? I cannot go home to my family. I am too ashamed. I am buried too deep in failure and regret. I don't know where to turn for help. Sally has made her heart impenetrable; she does not talk about feelings or emotions. She does not tolerate weakness.

I decide to buy some time, cling to existence with my fingernails before I let go. The only way I know how to buy time is to sell myself. I will do the bare minimum. I'll try to get tips at clubs. It won't be the big cash-for-sex money, but I know this is all I can manage. Scavenge for scraps and leftovers like dogs outside the city walls.

Our beloved country will "go to the dogs", the die-hard Rhodesians cried at the inevitability of Black rule. I have "gone to the dogs". I am ruined. I am washed up and washed out. Wash, rinse, repeat. Survive, scavenge, repeat.

I remember the time, just a few months ago, when Sally and I had driven around London in a limousine. Our neighbours down the road owned a limo service. They were twins; young Black entrepreneurs making their way in the world one limo trip at a time. They would often be washing and polishing their limos in the street. Double black limos, double Black gentlemen. Identical. I could not tell them apart. We called them 'The Twins'.

One of The Twins took Sally and I for a free ride once. We sat in the elongated black vehicle thinking we were somebodies. We opened the roof and stuck our heads out the top of the car. We turned heads; people waved. Some ran alongside, trying to see if we were anyone famous. I had felt untouchable, special and classy. I had 'made it', a big shot city girl.

Now I look around the escort club I am in tonight. I can hear Gecko saying in his Texan drawl, "Look around girl, you are sliding down the slope!"

I am exactly where he had warned me I would be. There is no exclusivity here. Men can just walk in off the street. The clients are younger. Drunker. Not big spenders. This is a place for tourists to gawk at the sex-world. Gangs of testosterone- and beer-fuelled boys edge each other on to embark on exploits they can brag about when their girlfriends are not around.

I find it tiresome. I am not in the mood. I can't be bothered to spend my dwindling energy with these loudmouth, inebriated slobs. This club is a waste of time, we are just booze-bait. Window-shop candy to get the customers spending money to buy us drinks. I'll walk out of here with my hostess tip of twenty-five quid and nothing more. It will not be enough.

I cannot fake sweet and coy anymore. My dark, brooding stare and sarcastic one-liners are not exactly drawing bees to the honey pot. Someone tries his luck. He scuttles away after a few minutes with Miss Buzz Kill. They are dropping like flies on a murderously hot day.

Here come my favourite one-liners. "What's a nice girl like you doing in a place like this?" and, "You are so well-spoken."

Men are surprised to find me here. I am unexpected, an anomaly. I am something to be puzzled over. The English have for decades used the English language as the primary measure of intelligence. I know what 'well-spoken' implies. It means I have jumped through the first hoop and qualify for the next round. It is not enough to merely speak English, a language widely considered the hardest to learn – you must speak it 'well'. This means without any trace of your mother tongue accent. Anyone who speaks with a thick or foreign accent is immediately deemed less intelligent, less competent or untrustworthy. They do not qualify for the next round.

One must pontificate and dissertate with perfect pronunciation. Ironically, English is over 60% borrowed, it's a bastardised language with words stolen from German, French, Latin and Greek.

My blend of Rhodesian and South African English is bizarrely close to the way the very posh and hoity toity speak. The upper crust of English society all say "ja", with a long, drawn-out 'aah' sound. Elocution lessons and private education have refined my spoken English. My accent has not been flattened by the Afrikaans dialect and I round out my vowels beautifully. How, now, brown, cow!

Society has ascribed its own set of stereotypes to foreign accents. The French, Spanish and Italian accents are romantic. The Queen's English, spoken with a hot potato in one's mouth, denotes class, breeding and intelligence. The Russian accent is associated with menacing bad guys speaking broken English in spy movies. Americans sound confident, are loud and opinionated. The Black African accent is the victim of the worst bias. It's the voice of despotic dictators, the stupid, the starving and the illiterate. As if the only way to have an intelligent conversation is to speak flawless and unbroken English.

My accent isn't able to be boxed. I am out of place. I sound decent, educated, composed. I sound posh around the other girls who are working class or foreign. I sound alarmingly like the men's mothers and sisters.

I can't play pretend anymore. I can't shape-shift. I cannot leave with anyone I meet in the club. I now know how dangerous it is. I can't do what I used to do to earn real money. My eyes are always searching the room for a stocky man with a scarred face.

Recently, I thought I saw him on television being interviewed outside a courthouse. I was curled up on the curved Edwardian couch, sipping tea. My hand started shaking, spilling hot milky liquid. I had to put the teacup down. I struggled to breathe. It wasn't a bad dream. The Boogeyman is real.

There is another image that haunts me. I try to shake it off, but it nags and gnaws at me. I keep seeing my future self.

I have been in London for just eight months and in this time, I have lived as wildly and as freely as I could imagine. I have flung all caution and sensibility to the wind. I have lived extravagantly, severing all ties to decency and feasting on every unsavoury pleasure and thrill-seeking opportunity. I have binged on cocaine, sesame-prawn toasts and all forms of indulgent debauchery. I have used and been used.

I have nothing to show for it. I am empty, exhausted and broke. I can see where I am heading. I can see myself years from now and it's terrifying. My future self is callous, contemptuous and heartless. She scrapes by, living on lecherous hand-outs and debilitating regret. She is incapable of love or being loved. She is broken and damaged beyond repair. She is most likely a drug addict and alcoholic.

I am just twenty years old. I have no future. I have nothing worth living for. I've done it all and come up empty-handed.

I am desperate.

There is just one stone left unturned. It's not even a stone. It's a pebble. A grain of sand. A mustard seed. A small voice. A whisper. A feeble little air bubble that works its way into my thoughts and asks quietly...

What about God?

CHAPTER 31

LOOKING FOR GOD
Sept '89

I've decided to search for evidence of God, the higher power. Does he exist? Will he reveal himself, I wonder. The cynical voice in my head tells me not to hold my breath. Why would God care about me? It's far-fetched and improbable that God would even listen to my prayers. I just want to make sure I have covered all my bases, considered all my options. I need to be unwavering in my belief there is nothing left to hope for. It seems prudent to eliminate God's existence before I end mine. I have no idea where to start.

I have very tentatively and awkwardly asked God to show me if he is real. I have also asked him to take me to his people. His real people, not the fake or flaky ones and especially not the judgemental 'holier-than-thou' kind, not the ones filled with self-righteousness. I have met enough of those and find them insufferable.

I ride the trains and aimlessly walk the streets. I pass church building after church building and nothing is stirred. I hear no voices. I see no visions. I look at the stone-clad, steepled church towers and they look empty and soulless to me.

It doesn't even cross my mind to find Joshua. He is from another lifetime. I lost respect for him once I had slept with him. It would be another humiliation to crawl back to him for help. I want rock-solid unshakeable, sword-of truth-wielding, salt of the earth Christians.

God, where are your people?

I have a few days left till Sunday morning and I have decided to go to church. I just don't know where. I'll get up and wander around until I see or hear something or someone calling to me. I'll keep looking for a sign. I don't know exactly what I am looking for, I just hope I'll know when I've found it. It's a vague plan but it's all I can come up with right now.

On Friday morning, I leave home for my day job, another day of sales defeat. Its only purpose is to fill empty hours and make the lonely days pass a little quicker. This little Acorn office with its whiteboards and trays of 'sales leads to call' has become an unlikely sanctuary.

The phone rings. It's Sally. She never contacts me at work. She is talking fast and sounds agitated. It takes me a few seconds to comprehend what she is saying and for the words to sink in.

"Gecko came over to the apartment to visit ... it seemed like the right time ... you weren't there."

I am trying to follow her gabble.

"I decided to go ahead with our plan. I told Gecko you are going to blackmail him."

The information filters through my ears, into my brain and to every nerve and cell in my body and delivers its calamitous message. This is not good. This is not good at all. This is very, very bad. How had I ever thought this was a genius idea?

Sally is still talking. I am trying to keep up, but my ears are ringing, and my mouth is dry. She says what I know already. "He is furious! He completely lost his mind. I have never seen him like that.

It scared the shit out of me. He says he is going to KILL YOU! I think he really means it. Listen, I don't think you should come back to the flat."

Shit, shit, shit, shit.

What a nightmare. I am in a real predicament. I have nowhere else to go. I have no other friends to call. I have to go back to the apartment. I have no choice.

En route I keep turning around to see if I am being followed. I watch the cars parked along our street and make sure no one is waiting in them. I lock myself in my room and wait, straining to hear any sounds of an intruder. Sally is not home. What do I do next? I am now literally hoping for a miracle.

Saturday, I leave the flat and roam like a stray dog searching for its owner in a sea of legs. I keep looking at people for signs that they are one of God's anointed. I am back to smiling manically at strangers on the bus or train like the day I arrived.

I had the whole year stretched out ahead of me with dazzling possibilities and travel adventure on the horizon. Now I am pacing around the city to avoid a furious diamond smuggler who thinks I am planning to blackmail him and who wants to kill me.

In a city with a population of nearly 7 million people, I am looking for a true believer, someone to throw me a lifeline. How hard can it be to find a good Samaritan?

Eventually I go back to my neighbourhood but decide to hang out with Tweedledum in his basement flat a few doors down from the penthouse. Just to be safe. He offers me some weed. I decline. I have tried it before; it had no effect on me. I need my wits about me.

He suggests we play a game of squash at Finsbury Sports Centre. I am grateful for the distraction. There are worse things I could do while waiting to be assassinated. Gecko would never do any dirty work himself. He would hire a gun. I now know how easy it is to get lost in dark alleys with monsters. I block out images of my skinny white body being fished out of the River Thames.

I am a competent squash player. I inherited an eye for the ball and natural ability from my dad. After an hour of 'thwacks' and takkies squeaking on the floor, I am sweaty and victorious.

Tweedledum is sulking. He has not taken defeat by a girl well. I leave him looking forlorn and burst into the ladies changing rooms. His bruised ego has annoyed me more than it should have. I notice two young women chatting on the other side of the room.

I march up to them and ask, "Is there a women's squash league at this club? I just thrashed this guy, and he is acting like a baby. Men and their egos!"

The blonde girl laughs and introduces herself. Jane. It feels nice to be out doing something active on a Saturday night. I like chatting to the girls in the change room. Jane starts telling me about a South African guy she knows.

"Steve is such a great guy," she says. "You should meet him."

I have no interest in a South African boy. I am in London because I ran away from one!

"He comes to our church," she adds, casually.

Penny drops. Lightning bolt. A sign!

Did I hear correctly?

"Did you say church?" I can hardly breathe.

She did.

"Can I come?"

Now, she looks a bit surprised. "Of course," she says. "Meet me at the Wimpy at Piccadilly Circus. It's not far from there, we can walk together. You can meet Steve."

I don't care about Steve from South Africa. I am thinking, this is more than a sign, it's an invitation. It might even be a lifeline.

CHAPTER 32

HAPPY-CLAPPY
Sept '89

I need to be outside the Wimpy where I agreed to meet Jane by 9.30am. First, I need to find something to wear. I open my cupboard and look at my clothes. One of my treasured childhood books by Dr Seuss is about a bear looking for a new hat to buy. The hats in the shop are too large, too small, too old, too new, too sporty, too silly. Nothing was 'just right'.

I flick through my wardrobe. Too short, too see-through, too clingy, too revealing, too slutty, too tight, too black, too weird. I panic. There are no church dresses. Can I wear jeans? I may have to keep my coat on for the whole service.

I stand outside the Wimpy. People swirl all around me and my eyes dart around anxiously, looking for Jane. Piccadilly Circus is in the heart of London. Throngs of people move through the famous location. It is literally the worst place to meet someone. Roads veer off the junction in all directions. Taxis and busses zoom around and disappear up Regent Street and Piccadilly. People mill around, but there is no sign of Jane. Idiot! Why did I not ask for the address? Her phone number at least. I don't know her surname. I can't even look her up in the phone book. There are busy roads in every direction. I have no idea which road leads to Jane's church.

A girl walks up to me and asks if I am going to church. Yes! What luck! She knows where it is. I manage a nervous smile. I explain I was supposed to meet Jane. She knows Jane and says she will help me find her. It feels like I've met another angel.

We head up Regent Street to the New Gallery Theatre. Most of the people who were milling around outside the Wimpy have started walking up the same road. We walk together, as urban pilgrims.

We funnel into the theatre. It's chaotic, noisy with chatter. I am reunited with Jane, and we find seats. She introduces me to a few people. It's a blur of faces and names. Just before the service starts, I lean over to her and whisper, "I hope this isn't a 'happy-clappy' church."

Until this moment, I had only had two experiences of church. My Catholic upbringing and a few extremely uncomfortable visits to a Pentecostal church. I am hoping this is neither.

Catholic church was dignified and full of rituals that could make me feel holy and pious. Kneel, stand, sit, sign the cross, say a 'Hail Mary'. Open my mouth for the holy communion wafer and hope my sins dissolve as easily as the white morsel on my tongue. Singing was sombre and subdued, except for when Sister Theresa's quivering soprano soared shrilly over our heads, not quite in time with the organ. Dad called it all 'Pomp and Splendour' and said emphatically that "God lives in the Kalahari".

The alternative was worse. My visit to a Pentecostal church at the age of fourteen was so alarming I ran out and waited in the car park, pretending I was feeling sick. People were putting their hands in the air and closing their eyes and muttering like they were in a trance. Some fell over, fainting from the Holy Spirit. All the clapping and 'hallelujahs' were undignified. I was very suspicious. Jesus freaks at a hand-waving show or altars, Hail Marys and incense? Both had felt phoney to me.

The singing starts. So does the clapping. Something is different. It cuts through all my religious neurosis and touches my pounding heart. The songs are sung a cappella, and only the sound of voices fill the old theatre hall. It is beautiful. It is deeply moving. I blink hard, feeling the tears prickling, knowing that a well of loss, of regret, of hurt, of failure and fear is going to spill out of me. I am unable to stop it.

Helpless against the torrent of all the suppressed and swallowed shame, tears spill down my cheeks. There is nothing I can do to hold them in. I look down and try to avoid eye contact, but Jane has noticed and reaches out to squeeze my shoulder and mouths, "Are you okay?" I nod.

I am not okay.

The speaker approaches the podium. Minister? Preacher? Evangelist? The title of the sermon is "Are you sick or are you dying?"

I know the answer.

I am not sick.

I am not dying.

I am dead.

I am certain I stand at the gates of hell, a rotting corpse with putrid flesh hanging from my bones, flames licking my ankles. Is it too late? Am I beyond redemption? Can I be snatched from the flames? Can I be brought back to life?

I remember the story of Lazarus. He lay in a dark tomb, wrapped in burial cloth for four days. Dead as can be. Irrefutably dead. From the moment his heart stopped beating, decomposition and decay would have rapidly spread through his human flesh. By day four, microbes would have been eating their way through his organs, emitting foul-smelling gases and bloating his body.

If Jesus raised *him* from the dead, I start to reason with myself, then anyone can be brought back to life. This is enough to pin my hope on and hope is all I need, a pin prick of light in a dark tomb. Jesus can raise the dead. I need a resurrection.

After the service I ask Jane if we can talk. She suggests we go back down to the Wimpy. I tell my story to her, a stranger I met in a change room only the night before. I say the words out loud that mark the chalk outline of my dead body. Every word of shame and fear, my vile deeds, my failure and my blackmail predicament are poured out in the fast-food booth confessional. Tears splash onto the Formica table. I blow my nose into wads of Wimpy serviettes. Jane keeps her composure and shows concern. If she is overwhelmed or disgusted, she does not show it. She needs advice from a more experienced person and asks if she can explain my situation to her mentor who is lunching at the Wimpy in another booth. I nod. I await my verdict.

She comes back and tells me what I know is true. I am in danger. I cannot stay in the penthouse with Sally. I need both spiritual and practical help.

In an act of incredible mercy, compassion and kindness, both are offered. I do not hesitate. I do not look back. I take the lifeline with both hands and hold on tightly with everything I have. Jane shows me something in the Bible. I have never seen anyone take out a Bible in a public place before. It feels more illicit than a line of coke.

She reads, "'I know the plans I have for you,' declares the Lord, 'plans to prosper you and not to harm you, plans to give you hope and a future. Then you will call on me and come and pray to me, and I will listen to you. You will seek me and find me when you seek me with all your heart. I will be found by you,' declares the Lord."

It is as if these words have been waiting for this day and this moment to be read to me. It feels as if God himself is saying these words just for me to hear. He has heard my prayer. He knows I have no future and I have no hope. He knows I am afraid of being harmed. He knows I am looking for him, searching for another way. I called. And see, God came running.

I say goodbye to Jane and go back to the flat. Sally is sleeping. I pull out my suitcase. I stuff it with the clothes and belongings I think I will need and leave the rest. I ditch the lingerie and knee-high boots, my long black wig which now looks frizzy and tatty in the daylight.

I leave piles of Vogue magazines, glossy pages I had tried to distract myself with in empty hours. I write a note, struggling to find the words and simply write: "I'm leaving." I drag my suitcase down the stairs and walk down the road to Angel station and get on the train.

I never see Sally again.

I do not look back.

CHAPTER 33

HOLLOWAY ROAD
Sept '89

I arrive at Hercules Street, off Holloway Road, with just a suitcase. I am relying on the kindness of a young woman whom I've only just met. I panic, hoping she has given me the right address. I stand in front of a narrow triple-storey house. The door is painted white. I knock and am relieved when Jane opens the door to let me in. I walk into a cluttered hallway which leads into a sitting room, dining area and kitchen. It's one long room that can be sectioned off with concertina doors, which fold back like tall wooden books stacked against the walls. The furniture is shabby and mismatched.

Jane puts the kettle on to make tea. Tea is more than a social drink. It is the way the English deal with broken hearts, grazed knees, calamities, grief and good news.

The house is shared with three other church girls, who are all students. Over the next few hours, they will trickle home, and I will meet the rest of the gang – Polly, Sandra and Jemima. Polly is from Australia. She wears her hair bottle-died red. Sandra is from Birmingham. She speaks with a sing-song accent, which rises at the end of each sentence. Jemima is just seventeen, and from Nigeria.

Jane is English. She's tough and sharply intelligent. She is a natural leader. I notice how the other girls look up to her. I find out, ironically, that she is the captain of the Oxford University squash team and would have thrashed me, had she taken up my challenge for a game the night we first met. She is studying to be a barrister at Oxford. Impressive. The thing I admire most about her is that she is not put off by me.

The Holloway house is the antithesis of the luxurious Edwardian penthouse. It is a broke students' dishevelled digs. The house has two cramped bedrooms, one on each floor. The first-floor bedroom is furnished with one double bed, a single bed, a wobbly wardrobe and a chest of drawers. Jane has offered to share her double bed with me. The first floor has a communal bathroom. The room on the floor above also has a mishmash of shared beds. It has no plaster on the walls and is covered in hessian. The windows are not double glazed, and it is freezing during winter. There is a third room the owners of the house have locked and use for storage. Paint is chipped or peeling, carpets are worn and faded. It's chaotic and crowded. Roommates and house guests have come and gone, leaving a trail of unwanted clothes, bedding and belongings and there seems to be no end to the clutter. It is like a boarding house for lost souls and misfits, and I feel at home immediately.

Unpacking my suitcase is a group activity as we hold up my clothing items one by one to evaluate their appropriateness in my new community. I explain the slinky long white thing that looks like a strange sock is actually a dress. The clothing suspects line up and parade past, like ghosts of my call-girl life. There are gasps and giggles. It's too trashy to donate. I'll burn it. Set fire to the ghosts. I assemble what remains of my clothing, adding a few unclaimed items from the household's lost and abandoned property collection. I have almost nothing left but I feel unburdened and free.

I cannot risk going back to any of the places where I can be found by Sally or Gecko, so I call my team leader and leave my job. I phone Sally and try to explain to her why I left. I need to change my life, I do not want to blackmail Gecko, and I will not be coming back to the flat. Ever. She does not take it well; anger and bitterness fill the silence when the words run out. There is nothing left to say but goodbye. I feel bad but I know I must sever all ties to my call-girl life if I am to have even a slim chance of a new beginning.

We spend the next few days reading and discussing Scriptures. Jane needs to be sure the decisions I make are not only based on emotions and difficult circumstances. I need to be sure my new faith and hope are unshakeable. I need to find my feet again. I need to grope around feeling for new boundaries, to make sure they are secure and strong enough to keep me safe. Jane does not know that if she shows weakness, fakery or flimsiness, I will not be able to trust her or anything she tries to teach me.

I want the truth undiluted, regardless of how hard it is to swallow. I have a tough exterior but from the day of my confession, my hard demeanour and protective layers are beginning to soften. My defences are dropping and the tender parts inside me are tentatively coming out of hiding, like skittish creatures afraid of the light.

As I start to feel safe, emotions seep from fresh wounds. I am embarrassed at how easily I cry, how tears well up, soaking into soggy, snotty tissues. I weep quietly when my name is spoken in prayer.

Jane and the girls welcome me into their 'all-sorts' family and ramshackle home despite my nefarious background. It's such an unlikely sisterhood and yet I feel a deepening bond and sense of belonging I cannot ever recall having had with women. It is an odd band of girls who have seen and know the worst things about me and do not judge, reject or pity me. Rejection and judgement would be easy to barricade against, but I could not bear pity.

My pride and ego are still trying to take charge. Pride, always the hardest vice to eradicate, continuously mutates and has burrowed deep in my psyche where it rests like a cancer in remission. Though I know I am here because of kindness, patronising charity would provide an escape clause and I would probably have ditched them. Instead, they offer a generosity and richness of heart and friendship impossible to resist.

※

I need to find another job. My options are limited, with my 38 words per minute typing speed and my Introduction to Desktop Publishing certificate. In Britain, menial jobs are always readily available. Most people prefer to collect 'the dole' and leave these paltry jobs to foreigners. I stared like a fool the first time I saw a White man emptying the bins into a garbage truck.

I visit the local unemployment agency and easily secure a new job. I will be the receptionist and secretary for a trucking company servicing the film and advertising industry. I will earn £138 per week, £27.60 per day and a meagre £3.45 per hour. It's a substantial drop from £300 for an hour as a call girl.

This is one of numerous adjustments I need to make to rebuild my life, repair my damaged self-worth, undo years of self-centred thinking and insecurity-driven choices. There are things that have been lost and things to be recovered. Can innocence and purity of heart be reimagined? Can self-worth and dignity grow over regret-scarred tissue? Have any others been able to recover after carving their lives up into such dramatic pieces, into 'before' and 'after' – so clearly marked out, like railway tracks separating good and bad neighbourhoods? I grapple with spiritual concepts as if trying to understand life and death instructions. "Lose your life to save your life." These are not theories to debate around the dinner table, they are the words I grasp and cling to in the battle for my soul.

Shortly after I move into Holloway Road, I know I need to decide about my life and future. Is this real or just convenient? Do I really want to follow Jesus or is this just a way to crawl out of my rock-bottom pit? I am usually so cynical, a scoffer and mocker of all things 'Christian'. I have in the past been scathing and intolerant of those I deemed weak and simple-minded Christians. But now I find myself unable to scoff at the love and sincerity of my new little family.

Jane is no doormat or half-baked cookie; she is cool, smart and fun to be with. I cannot find anything fake or hypocritical in her faith. But, above all, I cannot turn my face from God himself. I know he has heard my prayers, guided me to his people and held out his arms to me.

I leave the flat and walk down to the gardens at the Mary Magdalena church. I've carried all my concerns, questions and worries with me and I sit on a stone bench and pray. "God, is this true? I know you sent your son to die for everyone's sins, but I need to make sure ... did he die for me as well?"

I feel so small and insignificant, sitting on the stone bench in the middle of a park. I must look deranged talking to thin air. I see an image of Jesus on the cross looking down at me. His dark hair and dark skin matted with blood, his face swollen, bruised and bloody.

He whispers as if speaking to the core of my heart, to my innermost being. He says, "Especially for you. I have been waiting and longing for you to return to me."

This is not a dream, but perhaps it is a vision. It is so real, a communication in a spiritual realm that exists beyond time and place. I know in that moment that God has whispered to me. I run back to the Holloway house, as breathless and excited as Mary Magdalena herself. I am bursting with exuberant joy and complete certainty that God does exist. His son died for me! He knows me by name, and He loves me deeply and completely!

The next day I am baptised.

※

I get up on Monday morning to start my new job. I know the pay is lowly but at least there are ties to the film and advertising industry. I walk from the tube station to the address and find myself outside an abandoned lot surrounded by a rickety wire fence. Inside the lot are several trucks and a battered caravan wedged in the middle. I want to believe I have the wrong address, but the trucks are clear evidence this is my new work premise. I knock tentatively on the caravan and am greeted by Peter, one of the truck drivers. He welcomes me into the dingy and dusty caravan. This is the office and headquarters of a thriving removals company that transports props and antiques to and from film sets and photoshoots. It could not be any less glamorous.

Peter is over six feet tall and must hunch over as he shows me around the makeshift office. He points to the mattress at the back. It provides a place to sleep for the truckers who are too tired to go home or want to nap between jobs. He shows me the stained counter with chipped coffee mugs, the only table – which will function as my desk, and the all-important map of London which spreads over most of the one side of the caravan and blocks all the windows. The empty lot provides secure parking for the trucks at night.

My job is to take calls and messages for the seven drivers. Their daily routes are managed by sticking different coloured Post-it notes on the map. I am supposed to look at the trail of notes stuck on the map and liaise with clients to communicate when the drivers will be arriving, where they are headed next and if they can do a drop-off or pick-up on their way.

I feel like I am coordinating a city-wide heist each day. I am to keep the radio on and listen to the traffic reports to factor in any major traffic delays in the city. Urgent messages are sent using the pager system. A short, telegram-like message is sent to a call centre service and is beeped out onto a small alarm-like device called a pager. The receiver needs to find a call box on the side of the road and call in to the office for more information. This is the most advanced communication technology available – bleeping pagers and a map sellotaped to the wall of a rusty caravan. I am the secretary, tea maker, logistics manager and traffic reporter.

I meet the truck drivers as they drop in over the next few days to collect their routes and schedules. They are very rough around the edges, have zero tolerance for stupid mistakes and swear like proverbial truckers. Peter is the youngest, most articulate and polite and acts as a buffer, shielding me from the other truckers' worst flare-ups. He is attractive in his quiet English way.

This is my first real temptation and I struggle with wildly inappropriate thoughts when he leans over me in the confines of the caravan. I am tuned in to the crackling frequency of sexual tension that sparks unspoken between a young and attractive secretary and her boss. Every instinct in me wants to flirt and seduce him for a moment of needy reassurance. I avert my eyes from the mattress at the back and am determined to be as prim and professional as possible.

Jasper, another of the truckers, has a mean tongue. He snarls like a chained pit bull, and I worry he may bite. They all operate on the fringes of society, are covered in tattoos and keep their hair, beards and moustaches long and their tempers short.

I try to navigate the complicated schedule, the larger-than-life intimidating personalities, and being a new Christian. It's like a reality show called *White-Trash Snow White and The Seven Truck Drivers!*

I cash my first pay-check and spend most of it immediately. I buy a new pair of jeans, a long-sleeved floral blouse with a Peter Pan collar and a pair of flat, navy Mary-Janes. I look at myself in the mirror and am impressed with how demure and virtuous I look. Jane is dismayed as I have barely any money left for food and other expenses. My financial management abilities are zero. Someone else usually pays for my dinner. Money has always been easy to replenish. It's hard to comprehend how finite £138 is. But I remember how much my easy money cost me and am determined to learn how to live in the real world. This is the narrow road and there are no short cuts.

Fortunately, my new housemates are used to living frugally and we buy a sack of potatoes from the local market. We will eat spuds, baked, fried and mashed for the rest of the week. At some point on our 'poor as church mice' culinary journey, a stew is made from a suspicious source that is later confirmed as horse meat. There is no built-in washer and dryer, so we walk a block to wash our clothes at the local laundromat. Wash, dry, repeat.

New members of the church are called 'baby Christians'. It is an apt description of me. Not only have I been born again but I am learning how to walk and talk, taking baby steps in my new life and faith. To find my way and navigate my choices in day-to-day situations, I am encouraged to ask, "What would Jesus do?"

The answer is usually simple – it's generally the opposite of "What would Terry do?" Layers of learned manipulation, carefully guarded defences and pretension need to be peeled away. I am constantly tempted to act the role of the good Christian girl, but I am determined to be real and vulnerable. I need to keep reorienting my spiritual compass. I do this by owning up to my people-pleasing, vomiting up my shameful thoughts and acknowledging my impulse to impress and charm. It's a relentless battle.

At night I have no control over the intrusion of erotic dreams. They seek to pull me back into a black pit of guilt and shame.

My greatest fear surfaces. When all the garments I have worn, like the shabby layers of a homeless lady, are removed and I stand stripped of all my disguises, naked and exposed, can I be loved? Am I enough without all my 'party tricks'? I don't even know who I am without the bravado; the smouldering vixen, the rebel, the live in the moment, greedy, grabbing, shape-shifting harlot in the bullet-proof vest that I have been wearing.

Changing jobs and lifestyle, cleaning up my mind and mouth, choosing chastity and renouncing deeds of depravity are easy compared to digging out the roots of my rebellion, the desire to be the centre of attention, expecting the universe to circle around my needs and wants. This is the battle I still fight. Ego versus Soul. The Ego takes, the Soul gives, nurtures and creates. The Ego acquires and consumes and yet remains dissatisfied. The Soul shares, cooperates and finds purpose in uplifting others. The Ego victim-blames and shifts responsibility. The Soul loves and accepts the unguarded self behind the masks of title and accomplishment.

CHAPTER 34
THE CLOCK AT WATERLOO STATION
Oct '89

Everyone at church who hears that I am from South Africa asks me the same question.

"Have you met Steve?"

The congregation meets in groups all over London and Steve and I have not crossed paths as we are not in the same area. It's been a few weeks since my first church service and NO! I have NOT met Steve. It's starting to annoy me. What is so great about Steve?

I have had other things on my mind and one of them is my relationship with Seth. I know I need to be honest with him about what I have done here in London, even though our relationship dangles in a strange place between love and friendship. I know I need to sever the swaying rope and free myself of my attachment to my first love. I must end anything that could pull me back to my past self and dependency on Seth for validation.

I am struggling to let go of the idea of 'happily-ever-after' with him. If I tell him the truth, it will all be over. This is what occupies my thoughts when I finally connect with Steve.

We are to meet under the clock at London Waterloo. The Waterloo station is named after the bridge built shortly after the Battle of Waterloo and is a sore reminder to French visitors of the defeat of Napoleon at the hands of the Duke of Wellington.

To 'meet your Waterloo' means to meet an opponent or obstacle who cannot be defeated. The four-sided clock, suspended in the main concourse, has become a popular romantic rendezvous for lovers since the 1920's. To 'meet your match' has evolved over time to allude to star-crossed lovers and not your mortal enemy. The busiest train station in London moves half a million people through its platforms daily.

Minutes after Jane and I arrive at the arched entrance to Waterloo, she spots Steve and waves to him. I am curious about this 'Steve' guy everyone seems so enamoured with and as he ambles over, I can see why. He is disarmingly attractive but the first thing I notice is his wide, bright smile. It spreads across his face when he sees us. It's dazzling.

We are introduced and he says, "Howzit!", sweeping me up into a big bear hug. It is impossible not to like Steve, sincerity and warmth just ooze out of him. He pays attention when I speak and seems genuinely interested. I can see why he has made such an impression, especially on all the church girls. I am determined not to fall for him. I resolve to guard my heart and keep my walls up. The church girls can fight over him. There are plenty more 'Steves' in South Africa.

We arrange to play a game of squash and hang out during the week. It is the beginning of the kind of friendship that follows sizing one another up and ruling out any romantic possibilities.

I am learning to be friends with the opposite sex, to engage without flirtation and games, without innuendos and seduction. It all feels clumsy, and insecurity keeps creeping in, but Steve makes me feel safe and I have a taste of what it would feel like to have a brother.

After the squash game, we sit and chat. This gives me a chance to get a closer look at wonder-boy Steve. He's not my type, I have already decided that. If I am honest, I don't think I stand a chance with him. He is too perfect, too wholesome for a fallen, dark and kooky ex-hooker oddball like me. I have been told he has been stopped for his autograph, often mistaken for 80's heartthrob George Michael. His wavy hair with its tawny golden streaks and his dark eyebrows most resemble George's. His leather pilot jacket, faded jeans and tan cowboy boots complete the pop star look.

I am distracted by his hands. They are huge like bear paws. I find them very sexy, especially when he pushes back his wavy hair that falls over his eyes. I tell him about my bout of chicken pox. I pull up my white shorts and show him the evidence. I point out three faded pock marks on the top and inside of my thighs. It does not occur to me this might make a Christian boy feel extremely uncomfortable.

Steve is leaving in a few weeks to go back to South Africa. A bond has been formed and I know I have made a lifelong friend. We see each other a few times before he leaves, and swap phone numbers and addresses, promising to keep in touch.

※

I need to call Seth.

I put it off for days. I know the finality it will bring. I know the hurt and pain it will cause. I know once it is done, I can never take back the words or undo the damage. He will be the first person connected to home and my life back in South Africa that I will tell my tawdry, shameful story to.

While in London, I have kept our worlds as far apart as the sea dividing them. Thinking of him always takes me back to my first love, to the time I innocently gave him all of me, naively thinking it would be enough to make him fall in love. I had tried to hurt him and then cling on to him in our volatile on-and-off two-year relationship. I have self-destructed and destroyed our chances of ever repairing our love story.

We have kept in touch through letters and phone calls and whatever we have now is built on lies. He knows nothing about my call-girl lifestyle. He knows I have been going to church, this is all I have told him since the last time we spoke.

After three weeks of anguish, I sit on the landing at the top of the stairs, the telephone in my lap. With my index finger, I pull back each number, listening as the dial falls back to zero until I have dialled the long number to Seth's flat in Pietermaritzburg. Click. It rings. Every part of me wants to put the receiver back down. My heart is thumping, my mouth dry. I am so nervous I have forgotten all the lines I have rehearsed and when I hear his voice, I fall to pieces, and start crying. Between sobs, I just say over and over again, "I'm sorry... I'm so sorry...!" International phone calls are expensive. Every sob is costing me a fortune. He calms me down and tells me everything will be okay.

I fumble for the words to deliver the crushing blow. The words will bring a savage and incisive end to my on-off relationship with Seth. The words will kill the happily-ever-after fantasy. I can tell he is shaken. "Just tell me. We can work it out, whatever it is."

The words gush out once I start.

"I have done terrible things. I have lied to you. I have not been working as just a drinks hostess. I have been a call girl. I have slept with men for money. I didn't plan to, but I just got deeper and deeper into a bad situation and didn't know how to get out. I have been in a terrible mess. I am sorry. I have hurt you and betrayed you. I know we can never be together again. What I have done is unforgiveable."

I talk until it has all spilled out. I can hear he is also crying. It breaks my heart. I sit on the stairs, clutching the phone and waiting for the fallout, waiting for his words to travel up the crackling line. I wait for rejection, disgust and retaliation.

He says quietly, his voice hoarse and broken, "I love you."

Nothing has prepared me for this response or for the words that follow.

"Come home and let me take care of you. We can work through this together. I am so sorry you have gone through all this alone. I love you. I forgive you. Just come home."

CHAPTER 35

GOING HOME
Feb'90

I am not going home to Seth or my old stomping grounds. Rejecting his offer to take care of me is extremely difficult. I need to stay away from the physical and emotional patterns I associate with him. I am paranoid that being with him will pull me back to my promiscuous past. I will want to find a short cut to recovery and sleep with him again. To find security in him instead of myself. I am hurt and angry that he took so long to admit his feelings to me. I cry hot tears into my pillow at night, my bones aching with heartbreak. Doing the right thing hurts like hell.

I am not ready to leave London. I need more time. I am still trying to heal. I need to establish healthy boundaries and safe borders for my soul and spirit to breathe again. I want to be the 'good soil' producing a robust and fruitful harvest, and not the soil choked by weeds and thorns. I do not want to get tangled in a relationship that might suffocate my chance to change my life.

Seth does not take the rejection well. He begs and pleads. He promises to go to church with me, but I do not want to be just a 'church-goer'. I do not want to replace one kind of slavery with another. I want to pursue the sacred, the divine and the holy without distraction or hindrance.

My hungry curiosity has found a new obsession to devour. I pore over the Bible, craving truth to feed my starved soul. I am not wired to do things half-heartedly. I throw myself into Christianity with the same zeal and passion as I did when I consumed the vices of the world. It's all or nothing. I tell Seth there is no future for us.

Steve and I have been writing letters to one another. He went back to South Africa before Christmas and will be studying at Wits University in February. His letters reveal a young man with incredible character, kindness to others and deep loyalty. I am touched by his concern. He could have moved on and forgotten about me, but he asks about my plans and offers to help me settle in Johannesburg if I do not go back to Pietermaritzburg.

I don't want to go back to small town sleepy hollow Pietermaritzburg. Big city Johannesburg, a place where I can start afresh, sounds like a brilliant idea. I need some time to save, get on my feet again and move when I am ready. I catch myself often thinking of Steve, knowing he is part of why I want to move to the City of Gold. My heart patters when I see a letter from him in the postbox. But I refuse to fall in love with him.

"We are just friends," I keep telling myself. My heart is still bruised, and I am afraid to let anyone in.

I am not sure where home is anymore. While I have been in London, my family has moved to Botswana. Mom and Dad are teaching in the diamond mining town of Orapa. Orapa means 'resting place of the lions'.

Kalahari Keith has found a dust bowl town in the middle of a desert to drag his family to. Our family outings to the beach had always started with trudging miles through hot sand until there wasn't another human being in sight. Only then were we allowed to lay out our towels and open the umbrella. It does not surprise me that he wants to live in the middle of nowhere.

The phone rings and I bound up the stairs to the second-floor landing, hoping it's Steve. It's Dad. Dad has never called me in London. Immediately, I know something is wrong.

"You need to come home. Mom is ill." Dad sounds sombre.

"What's wrong?" I ask.

He explains that the doctors do not know what is wrong with Mom. She is in the local hospital in Orapa. They suspect malaria or meningitis or some African virus that is attacking her body. She is in bad shape. She is not responding to any of the drugs they have tried. The doctors don't know what to do. She needs me. I must come home NOW.

I need to make sure I understand how serious the situation is before I drop everything and fly home. Is it really life and death? Once I use my return ticket to get home, I won't be able to hop back to London. Dad is adamant. It's life and death.

Dad has called on a Thursday evening. I book my ticket home for Monday and work my last day for the truckers on Friday. I do some last-minute gift shopping on Saturday and say my goodbyes on Sunday. Most of my wardrobe I leave behind, to add to the growing pile of abandoned and forgotten items at the Holloway house.

I pack my gifts, which take up most of my suitcase, and a few items that will suit sunny South Africa. I have bought Dad a huge bottle of the finest Glenfiddich Scotch whisky. I have bought my nine-year-old sister a porcelain doll and a box of 150 wax Crayola crayons. For my middle sister, who is almost 16, a glossy *Vogue* magazine and sassy striped tights that I hope will be a hit. For my mother, her favourite perfume, Clinique Aromatics.

I make one last purchase. I need an outfit for my arrival at what is still called Jan Smuts Airport. Steve will be picking me up. I want to make a good impression. I want him to think I am beautiful. I choose my outfit at Laura Ashley. I still don't trust my dress sense and decide I can't go wrong with the 'Little House on the Prairie' frills and florals nostalgic romance look. The shop's window display is filled with mannequins wearing puffed sleeves and flowing frocks, cardigans and bows. These look like the kind of dresses that good girls wear. It's not me, I feel silly dressed like this, but I am still navigating so much unfamiliar territory. Just look decent, pretty and not like a tart. It will be freezing when I leave London, so I will need to change into my new outfit on the airplane.

�

It is exactly a year from my arrival in London when I board the plane to return to South Africa. From February 1989 to February 1990, the earth has circled the sun once and everything has changed. I will never be the girl that stood bewildered at Victoria Station again. I say goodbye to Jane and the girls. Jane, who saved my life. The stranger who became a sister. I say goodbye to the city that sucked me into its bowels, spitting me out bone-weary and broken. I was lost and now I am found. In a few months I will be turning twenty-one and miraculously, I have my whole life ahead of me. God, please let my mom be okay.

Airplane toilets are not designed to be dressing rooms. I pull out my Laura Ashley outfit. A navy blue and rose floral knee-length skirt and coordinating peony pink top with covered buttons down the front. It's very pretty. I thump and bang around, trying to change into my special outfit.

I look down at my legs in dismay. My bean-pole legs are lily-white and sprouting untamed dark hairs. I packed a razor, just in case and I will definitely use it before I get off the plane.

I remove my skirt and top. There is more thumping and bumping as I hoist my leg onto the cereal bowl-sized sink and try to shave it. The airhostess knocks on the door to check if everything is okay. I know what it must sound like. It will be a disaster if the door opens now, and I fall out wearing just my underwear, brandishing a pink razor.

My legs and armpits somewhat smooth, I look at the girl in the mirror. Her dark edges have softened. Her eyes can hold her own gaze. She believes in new beginnings, in mercy, in second chances. She believes in divine intervention and things that cannot be explained. She is not choked with shame. She has shed her snake's skin and she is walking away. She is not pretty, but she is beautiful. She is the scandalous woman Jesus met at the well, she is the repentant prostitute Rahab. She is the woman who wept prostrate before Jesus, drying his tear-soaked feet with her hair. She is Lazarus raised from the dead. She is Mary Magdalena, free of her demons. She is every sinner, leper and outcast that Jesus touched, embraced and forgave.

※

As I walk through the doors at arrivals, I can hear voices shouting my name. There is a commotion. I look up to see banners and balloons, an excited bunch of young people whose faces I don't recognise. They are waving and calling to me. Then I see Steve. I see his big bear paw hands waving and his huge smile. My heart melts. He has arranged a welcome party! I am home.

It's a short overnight stop-over in Johannesburg before I fly to Botswana to Mom and Dad. There are no commercial flights to the remote town, so I fly on the tiny, chartered plane owned by De Beers, which also essentially owns the town. It would be nice to spend a few more days with Steve but I am urgently trying to get home to see my sick mother.

Flying over the vast, flat plains of the Makgadikgadi salt pans, I am reminded how small and fragile life truly is. I have been fraught with anxiety over my mom's condition since my dad's call just a few days ago. I have had no contact with him since.

The plane careens onto the runway, bouncing along until it stops a few metres short of the fence separating the runway from the Orapa game park. Flustered and exhausted, I make my way through customs and towards the carpark. Heat is rising in shimmering waves from the tarmac. It's hot enough to fry an egg on the bonnet of a car. Dry airless heat. Through the haze of the heat and dust I see a figure at the fence waving enthusiastically. It's my mother.

My mother has made a miraculous recovery. The doctors were baffled by her illness and tested for malaria, yellow fever and dysentery and also did a thorough investigation of her colon, appendix and other organs.

There is no explanation for her illness or sudden recovery. I am in disbelief. I dropped everything, flew across the world under great distress to find no sign of her imminent death. Dad looks sheepish. Did he overplay Mom's illness to get me back home? They have no idea how challenging the last few months have been, how I am struggling to get my life back on track. I wanted to come back more prepared, in a position to stand on my own two feet. Here I am, broke, stuck in a dustbowl town and now pretending everything is just hunky-dory!

We have moved so many times, like hermit crabs outgrowing small-town cramped shells. The contents of our home remain mostly unchanged, and all the familiar objects and bric-a-brac of my childhood adorn the three-bedroom house allocated to teachers in the C Block. The couches covered in Biggie Best rose sprigs that the Botswana sun has faded, dark oak furniture and crochet doilies, and the painting of the lady in the orange hat that we had thought was a valuable antique. It was not. Now she gazes at me with her China-blue eyes, reminding me of the time our hopes of a windfall were dashed.

Everyone is delighted with their gifts, except for Dad who has given up drinking. I am shocked. I was so pleased with my extravagant gift, thinking he would be thrilled with expensive whisky. Rhodesians were renowned for their hard drinking. Sport and booze always went hand in hand. How did I get this one so wrong? Being sober in another small town will be difficult. The only place for men to socialise is the pub at the Country Club.

My mother thinks I have joined a cult. I try to explain that I have not joined the Moonies or The Jesus Army, Children of God or any other strange sect. She is not convinced. She is wary of my radical views. She is emotional about me leaving the Catholic church. She does not want me to move to Johannesburg and has been conspiring with Seth to make other plans for my future. My parents adore Seth and do not understand why I have ended things with the man they already treat like a son-in-law. I am not able to explain. It would mean telling her that a mother's worst nightmares had come true. I know that she won't cope. Drugs, deviant sexual behaviour, criminal activity and rape are not topics to bring up casually after a year abroad.

There is a history of sweeping things under the carpet in our family, of avoiding difficult emotional subjects and of keeping up appearances. My mother and I are not close. We do not share deeply personal feelings or painful secrets. We are not best friends. Our relationship is strained and taut and disconnected. I am difficult, moody, prone to rebellion and defiance. She is sensitive and easily wounded. It's a relationship carried along by undercurrents and passive aggressive friction.

We are the third generation of strained mother-daughter relationships in our family. I am now walking a tightrope trying to be a loving respectful daughter and a devout follower of Jesus, but my rejection of the Catholic church and her plans for my future are taken as deeply personal rejections of her. My determination to move to Johannesburg and be with my new community is seen as my usual defiant rebellion.

※

My mother loves to sew, and I think of a project we can do together. I ask her to make me a dress. Clothing has always been a battleground, my outrageous outfits clashing with her lady-like taste. My mother is classy and elegant. Her beauty is classic, she ages gracefully. I hope to make a peace offering with posy covered fabric and pray for unseen wounds to heal.

Teaching in private education is like living in a bubble of microscopic scrutiny. It's a pressure cooker of stress to keep family struggles and failures out of the sight of elite parents who want only the best for little Jonny. I had assumed that I was the cause of all her stress and embarrassment. But there are things that I do not know or understand. My mother has her own unspoken trauma. Things that are not mine to tell, things I will only comprehend when I too am a mother one day. None of us has survived without the lingering concussion of war, the fractured loss and the disorientation of immigration.

Mom has planned for me to move into Seth's flat and continue with my degree at the University of KwaZulu-Natal, Pietermaritzburg campus. She wants me to pick up exactly where I left off and finish her dream for me to get a fine art degree and marry Seth. She is so committed to this scheme that she has already paid a deposit for my tuition. My parents are prepared to forgive my gap year rebellion if I do things on their terms.

I won't. I can't. If I leave and go back to Joburg they will not help me financially. My mom begs, pleads, cajoles and threatens. I understand that my plans make no sense to her, but I cannot give in. I phone Steve and tell him I am a hostage and am being emotionally blackmailed by my mother!

It's not quite Jesus' forty days of temptation in the wilderness, but after two weeks in the small desert town, I feel my fledgling convictions have been tested. My mother eventually agrees to accompany me back to Joburg and meet my new friends, see where I will be living and investigate the church to determine whether it is a cult.

※

Years later, my mother will tell me about that time she spent in the hospital, while I was still in London. She had horrific nightmares. Night sweats and excruciating stomach cramps would wake her from these dreams. Her skin crawled and her head throbbed.

"I knew the nightmares were about you," she told me. "I would hear a baby cry. Then I'd go into a room where there was an old-fashioned pram. It was small, like a doll's pram, but very black and dark. The pram grew bigger and bigger and as I watched, blood would run down the walls of the room. The baby cried louder and louder but I couldn't get to the pram. I was trapped in the blood as it filled the room."

My mother knew.

CHAPTER 36

FREE
The 1990s

On February 11th, 1990, Nelson Mandela walks out of the front gate of Victor Verster Prison in Cape Town, a free man after twenty-seven years in prison. His release is celebrated by throngs of jubilant South Africans filling the grounds and streets outside Cape Town's City Hall. He and his wife Winnie Mandela punch their fists into the air, a victory salute. It is the end of a dark and violent era and the signal that the dismantling of apartheid has begun.

It does not hold profound significance for me. I am not one of the throngs of people on the streets that day. I am nowhere near the townships where people celebrate till the early hours of the morning. I probably watch it on TV or see the newspaper headlines. I don't remember.

My own life is shielded and disconnected from the harsh, degrading realities that the majority of South Africans endure. The four-year labour to birth a new nation, the so-called Rainbow Nation, have been long, painful and blood-soaked. Civil war and faction fighting have threatened the stillbirth of Mandela's dream child. I live with fear of retribution and retaliation for the privileges that have been mine at the expense of others. Once again, Whites are fleeing the African continent in fear of Black rule and yet another country "going to the dogs". Some stay, hopeful that a new day is dawning.

Our church community is committed to being totally multi-racial. At its inception in 1986, a handful of missionaries from Boston, USA arrived in Johannesburg, determined to build a racially mixed congregation in apartheid South Africa. Six years later, it is still radical for mixed races to gather in places of worship.

When I join the church in 1990, it is a vibrant, diverse group of about five hundred members. I learn to sing the Zulu and Xhosa songs. Hymns and songs of freedom that have yearning and the cry for emancipation deeply embedded in the words and melodies. "Thula Sizwe" (Hush nation), we sing, "ungabokala" (do not cry), "Ujehova Wakho" (Our God) "Uzokunqobela" (will protect us), "inkululeko" (freedom), "sizoyithola" (we will get it).

※

My year in London has started to peel back some of the layers of racism encasing my own heart. Sexual experiences with a smorgasbord of races and ethnicities have not automatically cured me of racial prejudice. My narrow White world view has opened to let a crack of light in. I now know that loving my neighbour does not mean loving people that are just like me. My neighbour is everyone, regardless of race, ethnicity, political affiliation, sexual orientation, gender, age or economic status. This is just one layer, the paper-thin onion skin on the outside. It is merely a starting point on the long journey to recover from racism. There are a multitude of layers, but I am willing to keep peeling them away.

Apartheid ensured that you could worship with your White brethren in your White neighbourhood in your White church and love only your White neighbour. It is easy to avoid your hatred if you surround yourself with those you find easy to tolerate. It is easy to avoid hatred if your friends are all the same as you, if you travel through the world in the comfort of your own clique.

I have Black friends. I have friends that are Coloured, Asian, Indian and Afrikaans. I call them 'brother' and 'sister'. This too does not cure me of racism. I live with a multitude of races and ages in various digs and communes. We share bedrooms and eating utensils and bathrooms and secrets. This does not cure me of racism. I will adopt a Black daughter one day. This too does not absolve me of racism. These are all layers of the onion peeled back, revealing bias, indoctrinated thinking and the privilege that shapes my world view.

Rooting out racism is ongoing, a life-long illness requiring intervention, a 12-step programme and treatment, like the cancer of the mind that it is. There are blind spots and dead zones that I do not see. I think unkind thoughts, I assume the worst. I think I know better. I judge through my White, private-school lens. I negate your feelings and dismiss your opinion. I expect to build a relationship with you on my terms. I am sensitive or defensive. I react with irrational fear.

※

In Johannesburg, I gravitate to the areas that remind me of London, the arty, cosmopolitan and gritty inner-city neighbourhoods of Hillbrow, Braamfontein and Yeoville.

I need a plan for my life. I am starting over again with no money, no financial support from my parents and an unfinished degree.

These things have become secondary and trivial to my primary purpose.

I am hell-bent on 'saving the world' with my new-found radical faith. In Jesus, I find more than a Saviour, I find a rebel leader and reformer. I find someone who rejects hypocrisy and false religion. I find someone who rescues the forgotten and downtrodden. I find a man who gathers the misfits, the unlikely and the simple to establish his kingdom.

I have found a way to make sense of my life and my past and a way to map out my future. I was lost, now I am found. I was in slavery, now I am redeemed. I was doomed to hell, now I am heaven bound. These are simple concepts.

It is an ideology through which I can reshape my narrative. It provides the structure and boundaries that make me feel safe and secure. It offers community and comradeship. Our group is labelled as a dangerous cult. This appeals to my rebel self. Instead of filling me with doubt, it solidifies my loyalty to the group. I reason, if Jesus was persecuted and crucified, this is how true disciples are treated. I fervently desire to be a die-for-Jesus follower.

My zeal is fuelled by naïve idealism. I reject the lukewarm, pew-warming, watered-down gospel with the same vehemence I had felt towards those I had thought prudish on my hell-raising adventures. The pendulum has swung. It could be a cult. I don't give a skinny rat's bottom.

Financially, I get by waitressing and painting murals on the walls of cafés and bars in Hillbrow, Yeoville and Rosebank. When I work, I wear paint-smeared labourers' overalls and my 1950's vintage cat-eye sunglasses. My quirky, arty nature has evolved. My Laura Ashley style has morphed into a hybrid, eclectic look that is post-World War femininity with a dash of grunge. I shop at the backstreet stores in the alleyways behind the Market Theatre in the city centre. My favourite shop imports bales of posy and sprig adorned 'tea dresses' from the UK and sells them for a song. They are reminiscent of the 1940's but are often short, exposing too much of my long, skinny legs for a church girl. I solve the problem by making knee-high cotton bloomers edged in white anglaise.

No one else I know dresses like me. I still can't help wanting to stand out and be noticed. I pair the outfit with chunky boots or takkies. During the chilly Joburg winters I just add more layers, oversized coats, thick stockings and chunky scarves. I tie my long black hair up in a pony perched on the top of my head, so it cascades down around my face like a dark, silky fountain. Big hair is still a thing.

※

I live in Yeoville, sometimes cynically called 'Jew-ville'. It is vibrant and multi-cultural, with an influx of immigrants from Eastern Europe and North Africa that will in time drive out 'the Whites'. The house I share with an ever-changing group of girls is the last residential house on Rocky Street.

Houses on the street have been converted to offices, shops or cafés. Our house is a rundown but quaint two-and-a-half-bedroom home with Oregon pine floors and high pressed ceilings. I live in the half room, a narrow room at the back of the house with enough space for a mattress on the floor. The other rooms are shared – two permanent residents in each room and a steady flow of girls that sleep over or stay for a few days, much like the Holloway house in London.

The other four girls who live here work full-time for our church and so this 'ministry' house is as busy as a bus station, with comings and goings for prayer meetings and gatherings from morning to late in the night. It is not uncommon to find bodies asleep on the couches, the floor, shapes piled into the beds at night, forming lumpy landscapes.

There is one bathroom. A bath, shower, basin and toilet cramped and compact, with rusty, leaky pipes that shudder and groan when we switch them on. We have shed unnecessary privacy and body shyness in this space and we pee, wash, bathe and brush teeth together.

We meet once a week to manage household issues like phone and electricity bills that are always exorbitant, to plan for the chaotic week ahead, the comings and goings and use of the lounge for meetings.

The oven doesn't work. We don't want to fix it because there is a mouse living inside that we do not want to bake alive. We cautiously use the oven top and toaster, live on takeaways from Bimbos and Wimpy or just eat cereal.

There are parties as well as prayer meetings and guys from the church come and go too. We are careful to ensure modesty and propriety to set a good example in the community. This is a good Christian girls' home.

A café is opening in Times Square, a new trendy hub opposite our house. I am painting the sign and some murals inside the café for the Bulgarian owners. They try their luck, flirting with me and seem confused when I shut them down, trying to do so politely and professionally.

Eventually, one day, very obviously puzzled, they ask me in Bulgarian accents, "Vat iz zeez house you are staying in zere, across zee road? Iz brothel?"

In the greatest twist of irony, our busy household full of young, pretty, God-fearing girls has been labelled a brothel by our nosey neighbours.

The church boys are intimidated by me. I am not girlfriend material. I am blunt. I say what I think out loud and realise too late that I should have filtered my words. Gentleness and humility do not come easily to me. I come across as arrogant and cold, but I am afraid to be vulnerable. My self-worth has taken such a battering. I am scared to show weakness. I am still groping around in the dark for who I really am without the armour of seduction and war paint make-up.

I often feel naked and exposed, terrified I will not be liked if I am seen and known. It's hard for me to distinguish between having a fleeting bad thought and a dysfunctional mind, between a passing negative emotion and a permanently rotten heart.

When I slip and fall, I think I *am* bad, defiled, corrupt and disgraceful. Guilt and shame cling to my psyche. It's a long and difficult road, freeing myself from self-recrimination and regret. When people say I am 'weird', 'odd', 'out to lunch', 'unreachable', 'irresponsible' or 'hard', I am deeply wounded by the labels that pierce my concealed insecurities. These are the words that make me ask, "What is wrong with me?" I fear I will never be 'normal'.

To compensate, I set myself impossibly high standards. I revert to the child that felt loved because she was good at everything. This just sets a hamster-wheel trap for me, a vicious cycle of reward and punishment. I swing from joy to condemnation, but regardless of the emotional highs and lows there is always a bedrock of gratitude that brings me back to solid footing.

I wonder if anyone will fall in love with me. What will happen when they find out the truth about my call-girl past. Steve is the only guy who sees past my thorny exterior and weird dress sense, into my heart. He knows almost everything about me. He is my best friend. I dread the day when he finds a girlfriend or gets married and I will lose him.

CHAPTER 37

PRETTY WOMAN

I have finally started to admit to myself that I like Steve, that my feelings are deeper than just friendship. It's taken a year for my aching for Seth to ebb away and for my heart to be available again. Steve and I have been best friends for so long that I am not sure if he has any romantic feelings for me. We tell each other everything – who we have crushes on, who we think would be a good match for each other. He is easy going and likeable and always falls for girls that are pretty, demure and meek. It drives me crazy. I insist he needs a tougher partner, someone who will challenge him. He thinks I need a man who I cannot walk all over and manipulate, but I know I also need a gentle and patient man to reach below my bravado to find my heart.

We often joke that we would be terrible together. A disaster. We laugh, talking ourselves deeper into the friend-zone. We are jealous of the attention we each give to the opposite sex, but justify it saying we are just protective of each other, like brother and sister.

The truth is the way I look at him and feel when he is near me is not like a brother at all. I search for him in a crowd. He is the first person I want to phone when I have news. I am giddy with excitement when I know we are hanging out. I think about him all the time. I can hardly breathe when he is close or casually puts my hair behind my ears when it falls in front of my eyes. I stare at his hands as if God himself carved them from bronze.

When he leaves notes for me, I scrutinise them, trying to read between the lines for any sign that he feels the same way as I do. I have no idea if he has romantic feelings for me. He is naturally charming, to a fault, his charisma can be misleading, and all the girls look at him with big puppy dog eyes. I am just one of a bunch of girls gaga over Steve. Damn, I was so determined not to fall in love with him.

Steve's parents divorced when he was eight years old, and he grew up predominantly with his mother and two sisters. He is at ease with women, comfortable talking about periods and mood swings. He is casual with his affection, always with an arm around my shoulder or those gorgeous hands in the small of my back. Everyone can see the chemistry. His uncle and his boyfriend noticed the first time I met them at Steve's twenty-first. One of us will have to make a move and risk rejection or even worse, lose a treasured friendship.

※

Steve has asked me to go out on Saturday. This feels like a proper date and not just another hang-out. We drive in my vintage sports model mini. My darling first car with wood veneer dashboard, white top with a sunroof, black racing stripes and chocolate brown sides. It's a little gem, a collector's item, lovingly restored by my uncle and bought by my parents for R3,000.

Steve says we will be meeting up with friends later but wants to take me somewhere first. We park on the road in front of the concrete water tower that overlooks the campus and Hillbrow. We get out the car, and he says that he must blindfold me. Do I trust him? My eyes are covered as he leads me towards the water tower. He expects me to climb up the tower blindfolded. He has lost his mind! Steve is notorious for his pranks. I don't like heights. He promises to be right behind me to guide me to the top. The steel ladder is in the centre of the hollow concrete tower. It is chilly inside. I imagine all kinds of creepy crawlies and squeal when a cobweb touches my face or legs. Water towers are an average of 50 metres high. I am not measuring but it feels like I am climbing forever in the dark. The surprise better be worth it.

When we get to the top, he helps me sit down but insists I keep the blindfold on. I know that the ladder opens onto a concrete ledge about two metres wide with no railing around the edge. It is a student rite of passage to climb the water tower.

I sit completely still, frozen and afraid to move a centimetre in case I slip off the edge. He starts reading a letter. I can hear only his voice. Everything else is silent, the world and its busyness has melted away. He tells me how much my friendship means to him and how his feelings have changed. My heart is pounding like a jackhammer. He finally says he has fallen in love with me. I want to jump up and hug him, but I dare not move. He has made sure I cannot run away!

He lifts the blindfold and asks, "Will you be my girlfriend?"

Hidden at the top of the water tower are champagne and roses. A declaration of love and a grand gesture. He knows exactly what I need, no ambiguity, no games, no keeping his options open or leading me on. I am not dangling on the end of a swaying rope like I did with Seth.

We watch the sunset over the city and then climb down the tower back to the car. While he was asking me to go out, friends have been decorating my car. It is covered in shaving cream, streamers, and a sign at the back that says, "Just dating!" We jump in the car and go hurtling around the streets of Hillbrow with streamers and tin cans bouncing along behind us.

※

Steve does not know all the details of my time in London. I have hinted vaguely to him but am not ready to talk openly about it. I drop little breadcrumbs, alluding to a difficult and traumatic past. He is intuitive and senses when I am quiet or withdrawn that something has been triggered. He is patient and does not pressure me. It's too soon in our relationship, trust must be built.

Steve can be fickle and struggles with commitment like many offspring of divorced parents, and still has a few years of studying ahead of him. There is no rush to work through these things yet, we have plenty of time.

We are also committed to celibacy in our relationship. I know that if I kiss him, then I will press my body to him, my hands will wander, my desire for him will start a fire that I will not be able to put out. We establish boundaries that we are both comfortable with. I eliminate all the things that I think will start something I will not be able to stop and am left with holding his hand and kissing briefly, strictly no tongue.

This forces us to be creative in how we spend our time together and what unfolds, in the space devoid of sexual activity, is a deeply respectful connection. Romance flourishes. Walks at Zoo Lake, picnics, long letters, talking for hours on the phone, and going to the Top Star drive-in. The drive-in is built on the flat top of an old mining dump and the views of the city are as much an attraction as the double-feature movies.

We sit at the street cafés in Hillbrow and Yeoville, go to the all-you-can-eat pizza nights with our gang of friends. We share the enormous spuds with cheese sauce and toppings from the street vendor that cost just R12. We go to the bookstore that stays open late or the vinyl record store. There are concerts at the Market Theatre and the Botanical Gardens.

One evening, the Johannesburg Symphony Orchestra is playing in the park, and fireworks will light up the sky while they perform. We cannot afford the tickets, so we lie on the grass next to a nearby road and little sparks and flecks of ash rain down on us.

The Mini Cine movie theatre in Hillbrow is dirt cheap. Tickets are R10 each. It is not as fancy as the theatres in the suburbs north of Joburg. It is tatty and the ticket office is just a glass window booth directly opening onto the street. There is no carpeted reception area with upholstered seats or backlit posters of upcoming attractions.

Hillbrow is the suburb that never sleeps, pulsating with lights and city dwellers enjoying the vibrant nightlife. It's the one-stop destination for clubs, live music, restaurants, all-you-can-eat buffets, strip clubs, drugs and beggars. It's a grey zone in a black and white South Africa. Apartheid laws and legislation against sodomy are ignored and people of all races, cultures and sexual orientation find a place they can coexist.

The tallest landmark is Ponte Tower. Once an elite apartment block for White city dwellers, it is now deteriorating into a vertical slum. The centre of the tower is hollow, overlooking a concrete base. Its nickname is Suicide Central. Hillbrow is known as the New York of Africa. It's the place I see ghosts and shadows of my former self, pale-faced addicts and tarted-up hookers, a reminder of my lucky escape.

Going to get an AIDS test in the STD clinic in Braamfontein is a nerve-racking intersection of my past and future. It is the moment

I confront the reality that those few months may leave more than just emotional and psychological scars. I wait three long tormented days for the results in which I play out every scenario in my mind. A life with or without HIV. It is a burden I cannot inflict on Steve, and I will end our relationship. He has insisted this will not change how he feels about me and that we will face whatever happens together. At this time in our history, there is no cure, no effective treatment. I will eventually die if I carry the virus. I will not be able to have children for fear of passing them a blood-borne death sentence. I led a high-risk lifestyle, so this is not simply irrational paranoia. The result is negative and yet again I am thankful for another miraculous escape.

Steve is taking me to see *Pretty Woman*. It's the latest romantic movie everyone is talking about, starring the effervescent Julia Roberts and dashing Richard Gere. I am nervous, I know the subject matter. Will my reactions give my closeness to the subject away? Rich, handsome entrepreneur, Edward, hires a vivacious call girl, Vivian, to accompany him to some social events. They fall in love and must navigate their disparate backgrounds to find a love that rises above doomed stereotypes. It's touted as a romantic, feel-good and heart-warming modern love story. It grossed just over $463 million at the box office. I am curious to see the Hollywood version of my life.

The original screenplay, called '*3000*' – the fee the call girl was paid for her weekend, was much darker, grittier and had an ambiguous ending. Disney, through the buyout of a bust production company, ended up owning the film rights. Disney was looking for edgier scripts but '*3000*' still got a softened Disney makeover and a Hollywood happily-ever-after ending.

I am visibly moved by the film, seeing myself in the exuberant Vivian. But in real life, girls like me do not live happily-ever-after. There were no Richard Geres in my story. They should have cast Danny DeVito or another balding, middle-aged actor as the billionaire. In Disney fashion, the charming Edward rides up in a shiny white limousine, gallantly brandishing roses and a black umbrella. He calls for Princess Vivian and climbs the fire escape to rescue her.

I have not moved or spoken during the film. I have sat frozen, my cheeks streaked with tears. I tried to be stoic, to stay put together and not fall to pieces. Steve thinks I am weeping because I am touched by the love story. I am filled with a turmoil of emotions that I cannot untangle or find words for. I don't want to deceive him, but I am also terrified too much information at this early stage of our relationship could send him running. He may decide I am too much to deal with.

Eventually I tell him I had a similar life, dropping more breadcrumbs that lead back to the dark, haunted forest of my past. He holds me and does not pressure me for an explanation. Do I dare believe in fairy tales? Have I found my prince?

CHAPTER 38

MY BIG FAT GREEK WEDDING

May '94

I am in a dim reception room at the back of a barn-style hall crowded with bridesmaids and flower girls. In a few minutes, I will walk down the aisle. It's five years since we first met under the clock at Waterloo Station in London.

I am trembling with anticipation, nerves and excitement. My face is flushed, my stomach swooping with butterflies. I ask my bridesmaids to fluff up the layers of soft white tulle and organza. My mother made my dress, a whimsical peasant dress with soft creamy organza draped over tulle and a bustier that pulls the dress together, accentuating my tiny waist. My tulle skirt billows like summer clouds swishing over the tips of my satin ballerina pumps. I am clutching an enormous bouquet of tiny white star-shaped Michaelmas daisies, a wild herb which is a symbol of innocence, purity and true love.

I have yearned for this moment. I am deeply in love. Since my year of downward spiralling in London, I have kept my heart, my mind and my body pure for this sacred day.

When we became a couple, we vowed to God and to one another that we would wait for marriage to engage in any kind of sexual activity. It has been a monumental commitment and a long and arduous task for both of us. Our attraction to one another has been fierce from the outset. How I've ached to kiss him and be entwined in a lover's embrace.

We've had to go to extreme measures to avoid temptation. There is no doubt about our physical attraction to one another, our chemistry is electric. My five years of celibacy has been like engaging in an extreme sport. It has required strenuous and unrelenting commitment.

We've faced ridicule, disbelief and scepticism. "How can you marry someone you have not slept with?" and "Don't you test drive a car before buying it?" But I've seen the wisdom in rewiring my warped brain, regenerating my heart and learning trustworthy behaviour. I have learnt to let go of my reliance on sex as a weapon of power and control.

I've needed to create space and time, separating my 'before' and 'after' with a fortress of beautiful, sweet memories and victories over my darker nature, to feel whole and wholesome. There are still weak limbs, fractures and fragile places, viral traces of shame lying dormant until triggered.

I know the emotional intimacy and trusting bond we have created in the last few years will be the bedrock for our marriage. Every struggle and sacrifice has been worth it. I can trust myself again.

The demons no longer rule over me. Dark secrets that once loomed in my nightmares no longer paralyse me with insecurity. There is no way around the monolithic stigma of my past. Sex worker, call girl, White trash hooker. These labels, scurrilous and smeared with disgrace, are invisible tattoos etched to my skin.

Disclosure would explain my struggle for connection, my shame cycles, why I am sometimes distant or distracted, unable to focus or get it together. The risk of judgement and rejection is overwhelming and only a few souls are taken into my confidence.

I'd opened up to Steve with care and caution, not wanting to overwhelm him, making sure that by the time we were engaged, he knew everything. He is allowed to ask me anything he needs to know about my life. We have no secrets. There have been trying times in our relationship, where I have offered to let go of him for him to find someone who can love him better, someone less complicated, less moody, less difficult, with a less deviant sexual past, with less baggage. I would sacrifice anything for him, even myself. I want the best for him, at times questioning if it should be me. But our love has endured. He has chosen me. He knows my sins have been washed away and sees me as God does, made new and whole, healed and redeemed. We have managed to forge a magical reset button, a new start and a new life.

※

The song to accompany the bridesmaids down the aisle is playing and one by one they leave, until I am standing alone with my dad. Through a crack in the door I can hear, "I've got sunshine on a cloudy day," as The Temptations sing 'My Girl'.

The 'church' is a Cape Dutch style barn reminiscent of a Stellenbosch wine farm. The white gabled buildings were converted into a banquet hall and belong to the Wits Old Boys club. It is a country-style oasis on the campus, with stone walls and green trimmed windows and surrounded by oak trees. The paved courtyard features a pond and a fountain, where Steve and I often come for walks. As our relationship grew more serious, we'd sit by the fountain and dream of a future together.

Dad is wearing the outdated blue 1970's-style suit he has kept in the cupboard, gathering dust, along with his platform shoes. He refused to buy a new suit for the wedding, insisting this one still fits. I gave up arguing with him – he is infuriating, stubborn. He is usually dressed in his Zimbabwe boxer shorts and flip flops, so I should be grateful he has even agreed to wear a suit. His moustache is trimmed, his sideburns a little less prominent. He has a white carnation pinned to his breast pocket.

Dad insisted on driving me to the church in his friend's silver Mercedes Benz. I'd waited for him to fetch me from the house and he'd been late, so I taped a note to the door of my little Bez Valley semi-detached, saying: "I can't wait any longer, gone to the church, meet me there." I had waited long enough for this day.

As I'd already arranged two white Toyotas to drive the bridesmaids, I decided to just go in one of them. We piled the voluminous layers of tulle, the four-metre-long veil, six bridesmaids, two flower girls and my mother into the two cars and were just about to leave when Dad came cruising down the road. Apparently, the Mercedes had broken down on the way to fetch me!

I walk down the aisle on my father's arm. 'Unchained Melody' by the Righteous Brothers is playing. The song is timeless, filled with yearning, longing and devotion. "Oh my love, my darling, I hungered for your touch a long, lonely time."

I walk towards Steve, my love, my darling, the man I have hungered for, the man I want to give myself to in every possible way. The man who takes my breath away, who has captured my heart and cherished it. The man who gave his favourite jersey to a shivering beggar on a street corner, the man with deep conviction, the man who is not afraid of the wild, unhinged, misunderstood misfit me, the man whose touch stirs me, the man I feel safe with, the man who loves all the parts of me, the broken and the beautiful.

The man who sees who I have become and not what I have been.

The eyes of the congregation of friends and family follow me down the aisle. They are here to bear witness to our union, but none of them can fully comprehend the true significance of this day. This is not a mere formality, a banquet decorated with flowers and garlands, celebrated with rose-petal confetti, free booze and fruit cake. I have overcome insurmountable odds and waged war for my soul to be here. I was in the sewer, head girl of Vice City, scum, garbage, my life going up in flames. Here I am, with more than hope, here I am with a future. I am clothed in white, bridal-pure, unblemished in heart and spirit. Today is sacred. I have kept my vows to God and preserved my honour for my love. My Waterloo.

*

When I reach him, I stand by his side, facing the minister, and our bridesmaids and groomsmen encircle us. I look at Steve. He is beaming at me. Photographs will capture the pure joy on our faces. We are glowing.

I once asked him, "When did you fall in love with me?" He told me his feelings changed when we wrote letters to one another while I was still in London, but the exact moment he fell for me was when I walked through the airport doors. He said I took his breath away. He thought I had transformed into the most beautiful woman he had ever seen.

Now on this our wedding day, we hold hands and face each other to say our vows. I recite my favourite sonnet by Elizabeth Barret Browning. I have written it out with black ink on the back page of a small vintage book of spring verses. The words articulate a devotion both vast and intimate, a love binding all that is lost and all that is found.

How do I love thee? Let me count the ways
I love thee to the depth and breadth and height my soul can reach, when feeling out of sight
For the end of being and ideal grace.

My eyes are blurred with tears, I cannot see the black letters, but I know the words by heart:

I love thee to the level of every day's most quiet need, by sun and candle-light.
I love thee freely as men strive for right.
I love thee purely, as they turn from praise.
I love thee with the passion put to use
In my old griefs, and with my childhood's faith.
I love thee with a love I seemed to lose with my lost saints.

I blink the tears away and say the final lines.

I love thee with the breath, smiles, tears, of all my life; and, if God choose, I shall but love thee better after death.

My sisters, both bridesmaids, are red-eyed with tears. A tear has trickled to the end of my nose, and as I exhale, I send it flying across the podium. I try not to laugh lest more snot and tears are sent shooting out.

Someone passes me a clean tissue, and it is a damp, snotty ball by the end of Steve's vows. He vows to cherish me, to be the man I need, to lead by example, to honour me, to be faithful, to place my needs above his own.

We exchange the traditional marriage vows and our rings. The best man fumbles, the rings are dropped, scattering across the room. A moment of hilarity, then decorum is restored, and I place Steve's ring on his finger. It is engraved with the words, 'My Prince'. He places my ring on my finger. It is engraved with the words, 'My Treasure'.

I am no longer White trash.

I am treasure. I am cherished, his beloved.

"You may kiss the bride." Our kiss is simple, sweet and tender.

"May I introduce to you, Mr and Mrs Angelos!" The loudspeaker blasts "I feel good" by James Brown. Applause and whooping erupt. We are radiant! In a few hours, our jaws and cheeks will ache from grinning and smiling.

A moment before the crowd bursts out of the barn doors to shower us with petals and blessings, I reach to the neckline of his white linen shirt, Greek peasant style with full gathered sleeves. I undo the two top buttons and my hand caresses his collar bone. My husband. I belong to him, and he belongs to me. My eyes gaze at him, devouring every detail, wandering without restraint. Like pupils adjusting from dark to blazing light, I can look at him with a lover's gaze.

※

I have married into the entire Angelos clan. Steve is a third generation Greek South African. His grandfather, Paupau (pronounced Paw Paw) came to South Africa as a young boy. The Greek temperament runs through their veins. They are loud, exuberant, and at times overbearing. It takes me a while to understand that shouting, insults and loud arguments are standard ways of communicating. Genteel, witty quips are no match for boisterous, arm-waving shouting. Steve is easy-going and good-natured like his mother, but he is also competitive, stubborn and passionate.

Yaya, Steve's gran, owned a florist at the time and I had gone to the market with her and Steve's aunt to choose my wedding flowers. I wanted violet irises and acid-yellow chrysanthemums, and NO old-fashioned Gypsophila, commonly known as baby's-breath. It was the first time I had to navigate the Greek way. My family's quirks and eccentricities are more subtle. We are polite. I was taught that raised voices are rude! We are no more or less dysfunctional than the Greek clan.

Steve's parents are divorced. In my first encounter with Pops, Steve's dad, and his second wife, I had to duck as pieces of raw chicken were thrown across the room in an argument. Suitcases were packed and doors slammed. Steve was embarrassed, but this kind of behaviour was not unusual to him.

My parents have never had a shouting match, thrown vases or pieces of chicken, slammed doors or packed suitcases. If there has been any betrayal, I do not know of it. In our family, difficulties and disappointments are not disclosed. Children are sheltered and protected from marriage's messy struggles. I am affected indirectly, with a sense that something is off-balance, off-kilter. I know that there are things I do not know. The unspoken weight is carried around, nameless and undefined. If there is conflict it is worked out in hushed tones behind closed doors. No melodrama.

※

Dad starts his speech with the story of my birth – assisted by midwifery nuns – at the Mater Dei hospital in Bulawayo. This could take a while. He remembers how I looked at him with intense, dark eyes and a scowl. He rambles on and gets lost somewhere in the Kalahari. Dad is prone to telling long-winded stories. Mom joins him and together they recite, 'If' by Rudyard Kipling. I cry.

We dance our first dance; our bodies melting into one another. Nat King Cole croons, "When I fall in love, it will be forever". The flower girls run onto the dance floor and hug Steve's legs, he swoops them up, one on each arm. I could not love him any more than I do right now.

The guests dine and dance, the reception is in full swing. We sneak out, desperate to be alone. At the edge of the pond, I sit on his knee in a nest of white tulle. The light from a round lamp near the fountain looks like the moon has come closer to light up our embrace. We are lost in one another, lost in the ebb and flow of our intoxicating first kiss.

When we return, Pops has taken charge of the dance floor, bouncing and kicking to Zorba the Greek. It is played on repeat until everyone is careening around in a circle trying to get the hang of the steps. He is the life of the party, and only takes a break to change his sweat-soaked shirt.

We wonder when we can leave, without being rude. We complete the formalities, cut the cake, throw the bouquet and the garter. We say teary goodbyes and try to drive our trashed car smeared with butter and shaving cream, bags of autumn leaves and tin cans tied to the roof and bumper. Steve's pranks have been avenged by his groomsmen. Butter will melt from crevices in the car for days into our honeymoon.

I am flushed, tingling, taut with anticipation. After years of restraint, my body is given permission to respond. Every touch, every word whispered with warm breath and the musky scent of his sweat and aftershave has set me on fire.

We leave, still wearing our wedding clothes. I want to stand before my husband in a white princess dress on our first night together. We ride the glass lift to our honeymoon suite at the Sandton Holiday Inn. We kiss again, encased in glass while onlookers whistle and cheer.

Alone at last. Our passion explodes. We are hungry to know one another and to be one. I do not need to shape-shift or shut down. I do not need to detach or disconnect, to mask disgust, to endure degradation or to sacrifice my own needs. I can be lost in him, swallowed into our union, engulfed by his love. I can begin to learn the shape of my own desire, allow my soul to surface and trace the outlines of our bodies without shame. We are Adam and Eve in the garden before The Fall. Our union is a gift, a grace, a hallowed healing and the completion of my redemption.

AFTERWORD
June 2021

There is a wilderness embedded in my heart and etched on my soul, as deep as ragged erosion scars the landscape. It is tempered with wisdom and the taming of life experience, the healing tenderness of love and compassion. In writing this book, I set out to search for answers, to retrace the dust-beaten paths of my childhood, the churning swells of my teenage years and the crocodile-infested waters that spat up my near-dead body from the underbelly of London.

Why did I need to do this? Why exhume a long-dead corpse? Why the need for a painful and gut-wrenching autopsy? Why turn back to the places that I've laboured to leave behind? Why re-open a cold case? Why not keep the door closed, conceal the stillborn creatures in the dark? Why hang the dirty lingerie out on the line? Why risk condemnation and judgement? Why risk stigma?

And so, despite the fear of recrimination and judgement, deep in my bones it felt like the right time to tell my story. To relook at the evidence, to lay out the shattered memory shards and bone fragments. To take to the witness stand and examine the mitigating circumstances. To examine my unique DNA profile.

A few years ago, a ministry couple from Zimbabwe stayed with us. The husband was running the Comrades Marathon. We sat around the dinner table – me, the product of a White supremacist regime, and he, a Zimbabwean war veteran.

White woman and Black terrorist, reformed racist and freedom fighter. We had grown up on opposite sides of the Rhodesian civil war. He and my father were trained to kill each other. He was the Boogeyman.

What we found was that although we had had different experiences, the after-effects of the war were the same for us. We were both adrenaline junkies and struggled to fit into society. We both felt most at home on the fringes, in the dead zones. Beneath the melanin, we had more in common than most, an instant connection, the language of shared experience. We both carried the scars of trauma.

Trauma changes the brain. It recalibrates the nervous system, putting our internal alarm system on high alert, with short- and long-term effects on the body and mind. The human brain needs a story to make sense of trauma. It is hard-wired to seek patterns, it is how we make sense of chaos. Telling stories helps the brain reorganise the fragments, to reclaim our lost and broken selves.

Story is a mirror.

Story heals.

Story connects us.

It tells us we are not alone. It fosters empathy. Shame cannot survive empathy. Like bleach disintegrates a stain, empathy washes away shame. Through story, we walk in each other's shoes, along dusty roads, behind closed doors, in hooker heels, or white satin ballet pumps.

But the true power of the story is that I now can look back at my younger self with compassion. I can forgive her. I now understand her. I can reorganise the chaos and broken pieces into narrative. Darkness and light, before and after, defeat and victory, heartbreak and healing, grief and joy. I can look at the stillborn and deformed memories, the jars of sweet rain, salty tears and semen, and put them in order, catalogued and labelled.

I have also written this book for the three precious human beings who are my children, for them to find context for their own struggles, to be free to fly and soar, unstuck and unshackled from my shortcomings. For them to know that I love them so dearly but imperfectly.

I am no longer afraid to be 'too much'. "Here I am!" I shout from the hilltop, under the spotlight, out in the open! I reclaim all of me like Russian dolls that nest inside my 52-year-old body – the untamed child running barefoot through gold-speckled swaying grass; the young girl, wide-eyed and curious, dreaming of a magic carpet ride through the Milky Way; the gawky, punk-haired rebel teenager; the art student fraught with first-love agony; the girl who seduced geckos, tigers and stallions, who wrestled with a crocodile and survived; the broken girl who crawled out the gutter, with only a suitcase, looking for God; the fallen woman who wept at Jesus' feet, and the woman who found her prince.

Today I am living in a future that I did not dream possible. I am an anomaly, a miracle, and I want to share that change is possible. There are still some things that cannot be explained and in this unknowing I leave space for the divine. It is in chaos and calamity that our purpose is born.

By the end of writing my story, after examining all the evidence in acute detail, I can close the case. I can finally shut the door.

ACKNOWLEDGEMENTS

Writing a book is often compared to birthing a child. I like this metaphor, as a child comes into the world only with a great deal of assistance and support.

My pregnancy was long, the labour short and difficult. I am deeply indebted to my book midwife, Melinda Ferguson. Thank you for believing in my book and in me, for guiding me through my wobbly moments and telling me to PUSH HARD during the last weeks of labour! I love your passion and devotion to your book children and consider it an enormous privilege to be published under Melinda Ferguson Books. Thank you for your personal attention as both brilliant editor and publisher. You are one incredible woman.

Thank you to Kelly-May Macdonald for final book editing and proofing. Thank you to Wilna Combrinck for her contribution to the cover design and for the layout design.

This story exists because of the remarkable kindness of a stranger. Jane Whitworth, I am always overcome with deep gratitude when I remember your courage and generosity. You gave me hope when I needed it most. Thank you to both you and Polly for assisting with dates and names of places during my time at Holloway Road.

I have a sisterhood who have supported my healing, both from trauma and racism. There are too many to mention by name so I will mention a few that supported the labour of the book! Thank you to our neighbours and friends, Rokiatou and Khustso Masethe, for your encouragement and for our many chats in the driveway. Thank you to Cathy Krummeck and Brenda Mhlungu for helping me process my emotions with lots of cups of coffee and glasses of wine! Thank you to dear friends Duncan and Lisa Comrie for helping Steve and I navigate the impact of the book on our marriage.

Thank you to my family. Mom and Dad, thank you for all the help with family details and verifying childhood memories. I am grateful for the sacrifices you made to give us a better life. Sorry that I was such a rebellious teenager and now I am being a rebel writer! My decision to write this book has been difficult for you, but you have done your best to be supportive. I hope you will be as proud of my book as I know you are of me.

For my children, Michael, Sindisiwe and Luke. My heart swells with pride and love when I think of how mature, supportive and understanding you have been about me telling my story.

Finally, my darling Steve. There has been no one more directly affected by the birth of my book, and you have been unwavering in your support. Digging up my past has not been easy, but you have held my hand and wiped my tears. You challenged me to write as honestly as possible, even when that truth was so hard to hear. You are and always will be my prince.